Stage II Recovery

Life
Beyond
Addiction

EARNIE LARSON

HarperOne
An Imprint of HarperCollins*Publishers*

HarperOne

HarperCollins books may be purchased for educational, business, or sales promotional use. For information, please e-mail the Special-Markets Department at SPsales@harpercollins.com.

HarperCollins Web site: http://www.harpercollins.com

HarperCollins®, 📖®, and HarperOne™ are trademarks of HarperCollins Publishers.

Library of Congress Catalogue Card Number: 85–51017

ISBN 978–0–86–683460–5

19 PC/LSC 60 59 58 57 56 55 54

To my mother
and all the heroes and heroines who don't
have things their way, but continue to carry on

To Father Harvey Egan,
a gentle warrior who makes a difference

Contents

Here must all distrust be left behind; all cowardice must be ended.

—Dante

They knew they were pilgrims . . . so they committed themselves to the will of God and resolved to proceed.

—William Bradford

I shall tell you a great secret, my friend. Do not wait for the last judgment. It takes place every day.

—Albert Camus

1

RECOVERY IS THE GOAL

As you read these words, imagine how many Twelve Step meetings are in progress. In your own town, how many "friends of Bill W." are gathering around the Big Book, fellowship, and the Twelve Steps to bring order out of the chaos of their lives? And I'm not just talking about Alcoholics Anonymous (A.A.). How many Al-Anon groups are meeting right now? How many groups of any of the other 200 Twelve Step programs—like Overeaters Anonymous or Gamblers Anonymous—are gathering at this moment? After all, addiction to alcohol is only one of the many ways people lose control of their lives.

Let your mind fly to all those meetings in church basements, homes, clubs, hotel suites, motels, restaurants, or treatment centers. Smell the coffee. See the

Twelve Steps hanging on banners. Read the slogans on the placards. Hear the opening words, "Welcome, we are a fellowship."

Look into the faces at those meetings. See the craggy faces of those who have traveled rough roads, the smooth faces of the very young, the faces of the affluent and the penniless. Some of these people are still toying with their problems and therefore with recovery from those problems. Some are brand new. They have arrived with the same soul-searing questions that you, perhaps, first brought to your program. They have the same doubts, feel the same hurts, and suffer the same near despair that so many others have experienced. Notice the old-timers. They have chaired countless meetings, perhaps know much of the Big Book by heart, and for certain know the Twelve Steps forward and backward.

Listen to the age-old comments:

- "I can't stop gambling and it's ruining my life."
- "I am as addicted to food as any drug addict is to a chemical. I can't stop, yet I hate myself whenever I go on an eating binge."
- "If I don't stop smoking, it will finish me off. It's already making me sick, but I just can't stop for good."
- "My emotions are out of control. I can't go to the store to buy five things because I'm afraid I'll get the wrong five. I just sit home worrying that someone will find me."
- "Hi, I'm George. I'm a sex addict. I've tried to kill myself a dozen times. Life isn't worth living like this —hiding, running, in terrible fear all the time that 'they might find out.' This is my last stop for help. If this can't do it, I give up."

Millions of our brothers and sisters are meeting in big groups and in small ones, in fancy places and in dingy rooms, in well-established orderly meetings and in catch-as-catch-can meetings.

What's more, for every meeting of the "afflicted" there are perhaps three meetings of the "affected"— the loved ones of the dependent person. These people have come to believe (or *are* coming to believe) that living in close association with a dependent person leaves its own scars and produces its own dysfunctional living patterns. Listen in. They, too, like their loved ones, have tales of desperation to tell:

- "I know I am as crazy as he is. Driving around at four in the morning checking out bar parking lots. That's crazy."
- "Somehow, I don't know how, I always end up taking the blame and feeling responsible for her insane behavior. I am so full of guilt, I don't even want to go out of the house anymore."
- "I keep doing things to help him, but it seems like the more I do, the worse I feel and the more that's expected of me."
- "I'm past caring. I'd kill the son of a bitch if I could. That's how out of control my life is."
- "All I do is sit home and cry. I don't even know what about anymore. I just cry."

Countless meetings. Untold hopes and sorrows. Words so real, coming from people pushed to the very edge of existence. Some come in desperation, some in hope, some just lose and are looking for more—but all —the afflicted and the affected—meet in the name of one great cause: *recovery*.

Recovery

What *is* recovery? What is the goal or destination this army of seekers is marching toward? What is happening at all these meetings?

Breaking any addiction—to a drug, a destructive relationship, overeating, smoking, gambling, or anything else—is enormously difficult. Breaking that primary addiction—getting sober—is what I call Stage I Recovery. The struggle is the stuff of heroism.

If you ask me what Stage II Recovery means, I would say, "What happens after sobriety? Is sobriety the same thing as full recovery?" Many people find themselves on the other side of their addictive behaviors, better off, to be sure, but certainly not enjoying the happiness they hoped for. Their victory didn't pay off the way they thought it would.

As a counselor, I have dealt with addicted people and chemically dependent/co-dependent relationships for nearly twenty years. And for nearly that long I have been a faithful practitioner of a Twelve Step program myself. For the past eight years or so, I've been hearing more and more comments like these:

- "I'm clean as a whistle and miserable as hell."
- "I've been sober for seventeen years. That isn't the problem anymore. My question is, When do I get happy?"
- "I swear to God my wife has a black belt in Al-Anon. I *hate* it when she tells me I'm on a dry drunk. I'm not even sure I know what a dry drunk is. If it means not doing very well and hating it, I guess I am."
- "I'm a closet white-knuckler. I go to all the meetings, but I just never got over looking back and thinking about the good times I gave up. I know many recovering people who seem to be happy and have it together. I don't want to seem like a cloud over their parade, so I never tell them how I feel. But it's true—sometimes I get real thirsty."
- "I thought everything would be great when my husband stopped drinking. The truth is, we seem farther apart now than ever. He's dry, but that's about it. If

this is the quality of sobriety we're going to have in our home, I don't think it was worth the wait."

The more I heard those comments, the more I began to realize how often abstinence is mistaken for recovery. But abstinence from a mood-altering chemical, binge eating, smoking, or a specific behavior like gambling is still just abstinence. As time goes on, especially since the dynamic advent of the Adult Children of Alcoholics movement, people are becoming more aware that the *real* root of malfunction is buried deeper. And that it is acted out on the stage of relationships.

A primary result of all addictions is the loss of self-esteem and integrity. As we come to accept that fact, we also come to accept that *we are not our own sunshine.* So what do we do if we believe that but are still afraid of the dark? What option do we have but to look for light in another person? Enter problems with relationships.

If we are not truly skilled in making relationships work, we spin a thousand complex webs, suffer delusions, and make demands on others that cannot possibly be met. If we are not actively working to improve our relationship skills, we start learning to hide the truth from ourselves. If we aren't capable of getting the "real stuff," we get what we can, which is usually far less than we had hoped for—all because we have not dealt with the underlying living problems that limit our ability to function in successful relationships.

Abstinence and the ability to have a happy life are *not* the same thing. As one man said, "Abstinence is like standing up at the starting line. The race hasn't started yet, but at least you are standing up rather than lying down."

The Third Wave

Since its founding fifty years ago, A.A. has set the standard for the effective treatment of chemical addiction.

No other program has been so successful, or so widely used as a model for other self-help programs. In the history of recovery, the phenomenon of A.A. stands alone in significance. There are, however, clear evolutionary stages—or waves, as I call them—in the further development of "recovery wisdom."

The first post-A.A. wave occurred about thirty years ago when alcoholism was recognized by the American Medical Association as a medical disease, rather than a weakness of the will or a degenerate moral condition. From then on, the social stigma of addiction in general, and alcoholism in particular, gradually began to weaken in the public consciousness. Stereotypical certainties began to give way ever so slightly, and although this process of enlightenment is far from complete, suffering addicts today have an enormous social advantage over those of the '30s and '40s. Public understanding and sympathy have never been greater.

The second wave in the evolution of recovery was the discovery that alcoholism is a *family disease*. For at least twenty years, therapeutic experience has documented identifiable, pathological patterns in the *families* of alcoholics and other addicts. As awareness has grown, we have begun to look at how family systems work, at the role played by the "significant other," and at the family of origin. Once we began to realize that the "afflicted person" is not the only "affected" person, it became clear that for any kind of normalcy to be regained (or gained for the first time) *everyone* in the family system must be seen as either part of the problem or part of the solution.

The third wave in understanding the dynamics of recovery has focused on the scope and sequence of the recovery process itself, rather than on the downward spiral of the illness. By now, the patterns of addiction are pretty well known, but what do we know of the patterns of full, ongoing recovery? This third wave did not leap out of a cultural vacuum any more than the first and second waves did; it has gained momentum as part of society's growing desire for increased health and fitness. As people in general have become more concerned with feeling and looking better, recovering people, too, are finding it less acceptable to stop moving ahead after the primary addiction is broken. Stage II Recovery, the third wave, involves making the most of a life that has been rescued from obsession and addiction.

What Stage II Is Not

I don't want to minimize the importance of Stage I Recovery, which I define as sustained abstinence or sobriety. Without it, many of us would simply die, or at least remain so crippled that any further thought of "getting more" would be absurd. Obviously, there can *be* no Stage II Recovery if Stage I hasn't already been accomplished.

Like the crawling of a baby, Stage I is a necessary and marvelous achievement. It is an essential level of development, ever though it is just a beginning. There is more to working a recovery program than just sitting in a meeting recounting old war stories. And there is more, much more, for most people than saying, "Stop drinking and read the Big Book."

Let me also hasten to emphasize that Stage II is not for people who think they have "outgrown" the Twelve Steps. *It is not possible to outgrow the Twelve Steps.* The spiritual wisdom embodied in the Twelve Steps is infinite. But, as the program teaches, *the Steps can only take us as far as we allow them to take us.* And, as in so many areas of our lives, we are usually only willing to go so far. Beyond that, we tend to float, in effect settling for "where we are," because we don't have the vision or the will or the know-how to do any better.

Switching Addictions

A word also needs to be said here about switching addictions in the name of Stage II Recovery. The two are very different.

After some people break their Stage I addictions, they find themselves pouring the same obsessive energy and putting the same blind effort into some other endeavor. These objects of obsession then become just another way to hide from the real issue: themselves. Their limitations. Their self-defeating learned behaviors. Their character defects, which invariably limit their capacity to function in loving relationships. That is why these behaviors are self- defeating: they block us from feeding our real hunger for "good stuff" to be going on between us and other people.

Some of the most obvious and frequent objects of switched addictions are these:

Work. It is easy to work or stay busy in the same hell-bent way we practiced our addictions—full of delusion and denial, and with the same lack of control that characterizes all addictions.

Group/Program. Some people actually become addicted to their group or program. Your program and your group are wonderful, of course; you can't get well or even "better" without them. What I'm talking about here is blind, out-of-control, obsessive binding to your group or program. Your group is supposed to be a means to continued growth, not an end in itself.

Religion. When you make a god of religion, you abuse the very nature of religion. When, in the name of religion, you give up your responsibilities to think, decide, and act, you are not being "religious." Passivity isn't a sign of spirituality.

Sex. Sex feels good. Momentarily at least, you have the sense of safety, or escape, or winning. Since most people experience a definite high with sex, there's danger of addiction. What happens when the object of this switched addiction becomes an end in itself? At the core of all addictions is the lie: "This will fill the void. This is *the* secret. *This* is what it is all about." But when the momentary fix is passed, payment is due for buying the lie: an increased need for more of the same, followed by a heightened sense of letdown.

Food. Eating feels good, too, so it is a prime candidate for a switched addiction. When we use food to solve a problem or reward ourselves, we are abusing it. That abuse can lead to dependency, which, as with all dependencies, then becomes an end in itself. When that happens, we are no longer able to make choices about our use. We indulge when we really don't want to and have even made commitments not to. We eat even though overeating is detrimental to our health and well-being. We delude ourselves and we deny the problem in order to justify the behavior and minimize its harmful effects.

Neurotic service to others. All addictions are neurotic because they are perversions of normal, healthy impulses. Even the best and purest impulses, if sufficiently exaggerated, can have misshapen results. Serving others is good and normal. Neurotic addiction to serving others, however, makes us unable to take care of ourselves. It causes us to lose sight of the boundary between them and us, between what is good for "them" in the long run and what feels good to "us" in the short run.

Stage I Recovery, breaking the primary addiction, often brings with it a clarity of vision that's stripped of much delusion and denial. It is never very pleasant to see what we have done and become while we were in the bondage of our addiction. Enormous guilt, however, may accompany that insight and in response to that guilt we may lose so much self-esteem that we also lose any ability to be good to ourselves.

Abstinence may get you out of a bad place, but getting out of a bad place just gets you out; it is not the same as getting to a good one. Switching addictions, even in the name of God or love or production or food, gets us no closer to Stage II Recovery.

The Importance of Defining Recovery

How do *you* define recovery? If you are in a recovery program of any kind, you need to know. Stop reading for just a minute. Take a little time to see what you come up with. Get paper and a pencil and write out your definition. In the past, I've discovered that few people I have come in contact with in any program had a specific notion of what recovery was for them.

How important is this? It's fascinating that thousands upon thousands of people are working at "recovery" without a clear idea of what it is. It's like going to a travel agent for an airline ticket, being asked where you want to go, and answering, "Away from here." If that sounds simplistic, look back at how *you* defined recovery. How focused and definite was your answer?

In my workshops, I usually get a lot of frowning and fidgeting when I ask for definitions of recovery. When people finally get answers out, they tend to say things like "serenity," "peace of mind," "liking myself," or "getting control of my life." But these responses are far too general to build a program on. In fact, they aren't answers at all, but questions posed as statements. To continue the airline example, it's like describing your destination as "someplace warm." You just can't get a ticket that way.

To go further, you need to ask some specific, focused questions. What would give you serenity? What has robbed you of serenity in the past? What, for you, would constitute peace of mind? Why don't you have peace of mind now? Is perfect peace of mind possible? Why don't you like yourself? If you had "control of your life," would you really be happy, or just less worried about losing that precious control? Is it really your own life you want to control—or is it someone else's?

So I suggest that you don't quickly run past these questions: What does recovery mean to you? Where do you want to go? Think about them and write your answers down. If there is no clear, simple, specific answer readily at hand, then consider that just maybe you don't know where you want to go in recovery. And if you don't know, you won't get there.

There *is* Stage II Recovery. There is Stage I Recovery. They aren't the same. They don't get us to the same place. We all deserve Stage II Recovery. We can learn to achieve and enjoy Stage II Recovery. But first of all we have to know what it is and what it takes.

How to Define Recovery

When we define recovery, we also define (1) what the problem or issue is, (2) what needs to be done about that problem or issue, and (3) what our program is for. *Your program cannot take you further than your own definition of recovery.*

Since few people define recovery for themselves in any specific, meaningful manner, *they have not clearly identified the central problem or issue in their lives,* and they don't have a good idea of where their program is supposed to take them.

For example, ask 100 alcoholics what recovery is and a majority will probably say, "Staying sober." Given that definition (that staying sober is recovery) then:

The problem or issue is . . . . drinking.

What to do about it is . . . . not drink.

My program will then take me to . . . . . abstinence.

But if drunkenness is the problem, and not getting drunk is the solution, then everything should be all right when the booze is out of the picture. You name the problem, you take away the problem, then you have no problem, right?

Experience deafeningly shouts otherwise.

Let's try another example. Ask 100 members of Al-Anon what problem brought them to the program and they will probably describe a painful alcoholic relationship. For them, then, recovery might be defined as "surviving the devastation of this relationship." Given that definition:

The problem or issue is . . . the devastating effect of alcoholism on this relationship.

What to do about it is . . . protect myself from devastation.

My program will then take me to . . . not being devastated.

If that logic holds up, then when the alcoholic in your life recovers, dies, or leaves, your problem is history. If the alcoholic's drinking was the problem, then you don't have a problem, do you, now that drinking is no longer an issue? Are you now "recovered"?

How many millions can attest that it just isn't so!

Now, let's look at someone who has a great deal of trouble with addictive relationships. Let's say she is a male-dependent woman who defines recovery as "not being dominated by a man." For her then:

> The problem or issue is . . . being dominated by a man.
>
> What to do about it is . . . protect myself from being dominated.
>
> My program will then take me to . . . staying away from men.

I have a number of clients who have followed this line of thinking. Sure enough, they often did stay away from men—sometimes for years. And those withdrawals were lonely and stressful because they weren't going *toward* anything, just away from pain. Often, the first time these women got into another relationship, devastation followed. Sometimes this was years later, but they almost inevitably found themselves in the same situation they had escaped.

Where your program takes you entirely hinges on how you define recovery—*you*, not your friend, or your group, or your sponsor. Think again about your own definition of recovery. Write it down on a piece of paper. If your definition of recovery is _____, then your problem is _____, and your program will take you to _____.

If you have to think very long before filling in the blanks, it probably means that you have *not* yet defined recovery for yourself. So there you stand at the ticket counter, not really sure where you want to go. If you don't have a clear definition, you don't have a direction. How far can your program take you if you're not focused on where you want to go? How far does any vague, unfocused notion get us?

The Dry-Drunk Syndrome

As hateful as this label is to so many people, it names a real condition that occurs when a person breaks a primary addiction (gets sober) but doesn't deal with the underlying living problems. "Dry drunks" can afflict people in all Twelve Step programs who have broken a primary addiction (Stage I) but have not gotten further into recovery (Stage II). *Victims of dry drunks have made a First Step relative to their addiction, but have not made a First Step relative to the living problems that underlie all addictions and ultimately limit their ability to function in loving relationships.*

The salient question is, "Why did we have all that pain in the first place?" Right here, we are eyeball to eyeball with the dry-drunk syndrome.

The medical model offers a useful example. Say that a patient is lying in a hospital bed suffering from a painful disease. To alleviate this pain, the doctor prescribes large doses of a painkiller. As long as the pain medication keeps coming, the patient has no pain. But what happens when the medication is taken away? The patient has a *lot* of pain.

We all use our addictions as painkillers. We do what we do because we are trying not to hurt. Perhaps at the beginning we were just curious or looking for a little pleasure. But as the process slipped from use to abuse to dependency, the addiction continued because it medicated pain, not because it was interesting or fun. The lie at work in all addictions is that continued use will get rid of the hurt. The truth is, it never does. It doesn't matter whether you're addicted to alcohol, overeating, certain kinds of people, or gambling. What do we have when we take away the object of that addiction? A lot of pain.

If you haven't dealt with your underlying living problems in any focused, consistent manner, pain, pure and simple, will keep you subject to the dry-drunk syndrome. In this condition, "I'm sober—when do I get happy?" is the kind of heartbreaking question so often asked. But the answer follows a different question:

When does real relief come for the suffering hospital patient? Not when the painkiller goes away, but when the *disease* goes away.

Unlike cancer or other diseases, alcoholism cannot be cured and does not "go away." A true alcoholic can never drink again; the disease can only be arrested. But the living problems underlying our addictions *can* be cured—if only we understand that dealing with those issues is where recovery takes place.

Stage II Recovery

Stage II Recovery is the rebuilding of the life that was saved in Stage I. How did our lives come to need rebuilding? In what context did all that pain come to be? Since few of us are hermits, the unsurprising answer lies in the social context—the world of personal relationships in which each of us lives and breathes and has had our being since birth. We get sick in the company of other people and we get well in the company of other people. There is no other way it could be.

I believe that learning to make relationships work is at the core of full recovery. While many people who have stopped short at Stage I may be capable of loving, they are not capable of functioning in healthy relationships. Doing so takes skill, and skills are learned. People may "feel" love but the reality of love is lived out in the context of a relationship, or it remains just a feeling.

Learning to Make Relationships Work

How good are you at relationships? Exclusive, adult, sexual relationships are obviously not the only concern here. I am also speaking of the ability to share in healthy, rewarding relationships with, first of all, yourself, your God as you understand God to be, your children, your parents, your friends, and your co-workers. Any and all relationships. How able are you to get the "good stuff" that all of us are looking for? How do you know how able you are?

The first step in engineering healthy relationships is to look at yourself so you can deal with the living problems that underlie addiction. In other words, you are not doing two different things when you deal with your living problems and when you work to become a more able and trustworthy partner in your relationships. *They are the same journey.*

From a Stage II Recovery standpoint, there is scant difference between an abstaining chemically dependent and a co-dependent person. Both are people with living problems. From a recovery standpoint, both chemical dependency and co-dependency have to do with *intimacy* far more than they do with alcoholics or alcohol, and intimacy issues are always about the ability to function in relationships.

All recovering people have to work on their self-esteem. And people with low self-esteem have a terrible time believing they deserve anything good. They feel they have messed up and deserve whatever rotten fate befalls them.

The truth, of course, is that whatever we think about, we bring about. Since no doubt the best thing that can be enjoyed in a person's life is love (which always comes in the context of a relationship), people with low self-esteem will always find a way to short- circuit or sabotage rewarding relationships. The real problem for most recovering people is not fear of failure, which we all know about and expect. The real problem is fear of success, and the solution is to get out of our own way so the riches of full recovery can be enjoyed. This is true not only for all recovering people, but for everyone.

The problem is not that we want too much, but that we have too little belief in what is possible for us.

Once the primary addiction is broken, we are all in the same boat because then we're called upon to deal with those habits, traits, and patterns within ourselves that stand in the way of our achieving more happiness, success, and love.

Therefore, let us work with these definitions of both chemically and co-dependent people. Remember these definitions are only valid from a Stage II Recovery standpoint, where the ability to express and receive love is the central issue:

Chemical Dependency: self-defeating learned *behaviors*, greatly exaggerated and complicated by a pathological relationship to a mood-altering *substance*, that diminish our capacity to initiate or participate in loving relationships.

Co-Dependency: self-defeating learned *behaviors*, greatly exaggerated and complicated by a pathological relationship to a chemically dependent person or any *person*, that diminish our capacity to initiate or participate in loving relationships.

Why tie up the definition of chemical and co-dependency (and the human situation in general) to relationships? Because relationships are the home of love, and the definition of Stage II Recovery, for everyone, is learning to function more capably in healthy, caring relationships.

Recap

1. An evolution in the process of recovery has occurred.

2. Stage I Recovery is breaking the primary addiction.

3. It is vitally important to define recovery *for ourselves* so that we will know

   • what the real issue is,

- what to do about it, and
- how to work a program to achieve that goal.
4. From the standpoint of Stage II Recovery, there is no difference between chemically and co-dependent persons; both must deal with underlying living problems that limit their ability to function in healthy relationships.

The degree of love I give is determined by my own capability. My capability is determined by the environment of my past existence and my understanding of love, truth and God.
—William Rinder

A choice confronts us. Shall we, as we feel our foundations shaking, withdraw in anxiety and panic? Frightened by the loss of our familiar mooring places, shall we become paralyzed and cover our inaction with apathy? If we do those things, we will have surrendered our chance to participate in the forming of the future. We will have forfeited the distinctive characteristic of human beings: namely, to influence our evolution through our own awareness.
—Rollo May

2

SELF-DEFEATING LEARNED BEHAVIORS

If functioning in healthier relationships is the goal of Stage II Recovery, then how can you attain it? What has been standing in the way? If recovery is learning how to love, then what is the obstacle?

Self-defeating learned behaviors are what get in the way. These are ways of thinking and acting that we have practiced and that, through practice, have become habits. In the course of time, these habits have become who we are. And *who we are* has become rooted in our subconscious, so that we now automatically act out these behavioral patterns whether we are aware of them or not. It is the power of these patterns speaking when we hear someone say, "I am who I am and I can't help it." In truth, the "I am who I am" part is certainly correct, but the "I can't help it" part isn't.

Habits can be changed. We can learn new ways just as we learned the old ones—by practice. We may not be able to change our nature, but we surely can change our character if we want to. Hiders can learn to come out from behind their shields. Stuffers can learn to deal with problems as they come up. Liars can learn to be honest. But we can only do this if we see the need to change habits as an integral part of recovery.

Paradoxically, the success of Stage I can be the obstacle of Stage II. It is a classic case of the good being the enemy of the best. In Stage I, our problem was so clear and our pain so intense that we were motivated to bear down until things got better. But once we had broken through the wall of Stage I, we hurt less. Much less. We'd found friendship and fellowship in the program. We'd learned to avoid most of the crazy-making situations we used to get into, and we'd discovered that we weren't alone. Since our pain was reduced, we tended to let down and relax. The issue of Stage II (our living problems) just doesn't seem as serious as the issue of Stage I (our addiction). After all, the issue is *us*, and our own hiding places.

It is only human to love our own comfort zones. And if the call to recovery grew faint after Stage I, we probably never came face to face with those self-defeating learned behaviors. And so they stay—inhibiting the growth of our ability to function in truly satisfying relationships.

Types of Self-Defeating
Learned Behaviors

Here are six categories of self-defeating learned behaviors. While this list certainly doesn't cover all possibilities, it does characterize a lot of common, habitual patterns. Perhaps you will see yourself (as I see myself) in more than one category. Or perhaps something you read here will give you insight into your own special style of thinking and doing. Be aware that these categories represent *extremes;* each one is the exaggeration of a healthy, normal impulse.

Caretakers

Caretakers don't just care for others; they breed dependency. Often from early childhood, Caretakers have learned to base their self-image on how much they can do for other people. They "baby-make" in the name of care and love.

But because they see their main task in life as taking care of others, they never learn to take very good care of themselves. And the "others" learn that they never really have to take responsibility for the consequences of their actions. Why? Because the Caretaker will always be there to set things right, bail them out, yank the fat out of the fire.

Habits create needs. So it isn't long before the Caretaker *needs,* subconsciously of course, dependent people around. If there aren't some dependents handy, a dedicated Caretaker will find or make some.

Not surprisingly, Caretakers get dragged down from time to time. They'll say to themselves, "My God! I don't have a single responsible person in my life. Everybody I know uses me!" Of course they do. If they

didn't, the Caretaker couldn't get much of a relationship going with them. So the real question isn't, "Why
do *they* act like that?" but "Why do *I* find myself in the
same predicament all the time?" Who you are in a relationship *with* says as much about you as it does about the
other person.

In Stage II Recovery, Caretakers can learn to stop
playing God and allow others to take responsibility for
their own actions. Life is so much easier when we stop
playing God.

People-Pleasers

People-Pleasers have learned that their self-esteem is
based on never making anyone angry. "I can never say
no," their thinking goes, "because if I do, people will
get mad and turn away from me. If they get mad, I must
be bad, and if I am bad they will go away. Then I will be
all alone. Therefore, I must never say no or do anything that will make people go away."

Chronic People-Pleasers almost never have satisfying
relationships because they lie—indirectly and habitually. When a People-Pleaser's spouse comes home and
asks, "How are you doing?" the People-Pleaser will say,
"Fine," no matter what's going on. She may be so mad
she can't see straight, or he may be so depressed he
doesn't even feel alive, but a People-Pleaser is always
"fine." Sooner or later, though, what isn't so fine will
burst out in a volcano of indirect punishment.

People-Pleasers aren't fine because they don't get
what they need. Many times they don't get it because
they don't ask for it and the "other" doesn't know.
They have given away their power, and claiming their
own rights seems beyond them. Rather than coming
straight out and declaring who they are and what they
want, they hope and pray that somehow the others will
just "know"—and, in knowing, "care." So, People-

Pleasers are always in a state of emotional starvation. And as they starve, they indirectly punish their others for not giving what they would not ask for.

Because habitual behaviors create needs and set up patterns, People-Pleasers often end up with abusers. People who won't claim their rights are almost certain to come across others who are more than willing to take their rights away from them. But the real issue for recovery has very little to do with *them*, and everything to do with *us*. If "they" are not considerate of my rights or respectful of who I am, why did I choose this relationship in the first place?

Wherever you go, there you are. If nothing changes, nothing changes. In Stage II Recovery, People-Pleasers can learn to assert their own rights and not feel apologetic about it. They definitely can learn to say, "I count!"

Martyrs

Martyrs have learned that life only has meaning when there's plenty of suffering going on; they court pain for the sake of normalcy. Typically, Martyrs become frightened if they have a few good days. It doesn't fit. Like anybody who gets frightened, Martyrs tend to revert to form. They find ways to make sure that things don't get *too* good. If their relationships seem to be rolling along peacefully, they find some way to derail the train.

People invariably accomplish what they truly believe, and since Martyrs truly believe that life is supposed to be a struggle, a struggle is what they get. Nothing is ever *really* good, truly enjoyable, or a pure joy. For Martyrs, the best that something can be is "nice." Habits create needs and Martyrs need to suffer.

Aggressive Martyrs often form relationships with passive, trembling types. Then they feel bad for having no

get-up-and-go. They can complain that they have to
make all the decisions and do all the work. But of course
that is *why* they formed that relationship. In Stage II
Recovery, Martyrs can become people who *do not need* to
suffer in abusive relationships.

Workaholics

These are people who have learned to base their self-
esteem on activity. I used to say that the Workaholic's
self-esteem was based on productivity, but I have come
across many Workaholics who simply just have to be
busy. Accomplishment isn't it—just flying around in
constant motion seems to be enough. Some people call
this the "craziness of the busies."

Workaholics find it extremely difficult to relax. They
need "busyness" to feel worthwhile and they are never
off the hook because their need to *do* is merciless.
Workaholic Martyrs carry it a step farther and feel
guilty when they aren't busy.

In relationships, Workaholics continually communicate to their "others" that while they may be important
they're just not *as* important as the project, profit, or
performance at hand. Workaholics are disheartening
to live with, but in Stage II Recovery they can learn to
feel worthwhile even though they are at rest.

Perfectionists

Since nothing on earth can ever be perfect, Perfectionists can never be happy or satisfied. The base of their
self-esteem is unattainable. Perfectionists live in a terrible bondage. Not only must the "things" around them
be perfect, but so must the people. They are absolute
masters at finding fault. Nothing is ever quite good
enough. A child who gets four "A"s and one "B" on a
report card will hear the Perfectionist parent say, "Nice

—but what happened with that 'B'? Let's see if we can do something about that." Imperfection abounds of course, so Perfectionists don't have far to look. They are just more skilled than the rest of us at seeing it, commenting on it, and allowing fallibility to control their lives.

Perfectionists (like Caretakers or People-Pleasers) don't fall out of the trees fully formed at age thirty. They have *practiced* becoming who they are. They were trained, then they went into training themselves, and finally *they* started training others. The cycle is clear enough once you start to look for it.

After Stage I, a clean and sober addict is just that— clean and sober. Alcoholic Perfectionists who gain sobriety are still Perfectionists and, like fleas on a dog, their tendency to neurotic perfectionism will chew away at their efforts to be happy. Stage II Recovery begins when we look at the living problems that underlie all addictions. Perfectionists can learn to live at peace with an imperfect world. They can learn the blessed relief that comes from accepting themselves as they are— flawed—and allowing others the same right to be imperfect as well.

Tap Dancers

Tap Dancers base their self-esteem on staying loose: they have learned to *never* make a full commitment. They got their name because they never stand still, at least emotionally. You can't get a straight answer out of a Tap Dancer. They are experts at creating back doors.

Tap Dancers don't often have just one primary relationship. Sometimes they have five going on at the same time. If one doesn't work out, they can fall back on the other four. Tap Dancers seem to get high living on the razor's edge. A deep, dark part of them seems to love the danger of getting caught. To them, life is a game of hide-and-seek.

Tap Dancers give just enough to keep the other enticed, but never enough to hold on to. They are masters of the half-truth and the veiled truth. You may think that a Tap Dancer has said something solid to you, but when you examine it, you begin to wonder. And the more you wonder, the surer you become that they did it to you again—gave you a "for sure, maybe."

Of course, Tap Dancers only relate to people who are willing to let them dance, so Caretakers and People-Pleasers are sitting ducks for them. The Caretaker may spend a lifetime trying to "fix" the Tap Dancer. The People-Pleaser will always think it's his or her fault that the Tap Dancer won't come out of hiding and make a commitment. So the People-Pleaser keeps trying "to do things right" while the Dancer taps away into the sunset of both their lives.

Tap Dancers who sober up can be worse evaders of commitment than before they ever started drinking, maybe because of all the guilt and remorse the newly sober person often feels. Guilt and remorse can convince the Tap Dancer that "if people knew the real me, they'd know all the terrible things I've done and what a terrible person I am. I can't let them know the real me!" So he dances away.

Stage II Recovery begins not just when you're standing at the starting line, but when you've actually begun the race by beginning to deal with underlying issues. Tap Dancers can learn to stand still and be counted. They can learn that commitment can mean freedom as well as confinement.

Can You Find Yourself?

It may be helpful to use the following profiles as an evaluation tool. See how many "position statements" you can identify within each of the six categories. Then take a look at the results. What you will see is some indication of the obstacles you're facing in becoming more skillful in ongoing, rewarding relationships.

Caretaker
- I generally feel responsible for the happiness of others.
- I have often "bent the rules" to bail people out of trouble that they brought on themselves.
- Sometimes I wonder why so many people lean on me without being sensitive to *my* need to lean once in a while.
- I find it easier to take care of others than to take care of myself.
- I never have enough time to accomplish all my tasks.
- I am more interested in talking about other people's problems than in talking about my own.

People-Pleaser
- I have trouble saying no even when I know I should.
- I often say, "It doesn't matter," when it really does.
- I seldom feel angry but often feel hurt.
- In the name of peace, I try to avoid talking about problems.
- I usually feel that other people's needs and opinions are more important than my own.
- I often apologize.
- I would rather give in than make someone mad.

Workaholic
- I rarely feel that I accomplish enough.
- When I relax, I experience more guilt than pleasure.

- I don't celebrate the conclusion of one project before starting another.
- It seems to me that people are in my way quite often.
- I put less value on personal time than on work time.
- I am intimidated by unfinished business.
- I spend more time, energy, and effort on projects than on relationships.

Martyr

- I am usually willing to do without so others can have what they want.
- I feel I have terrible luck.
- It feels natural to worry a lot about other people.
- My first impulse is to say no when something fun comes up.
- My second impulse is to wonder why I tend to refuse a good time.
- When life runs smoothly for a while, I begin to anticipate disaster.
- I believe that life is a struggle and I accept suffering as my lot.

Perfectionist

- I am often amazed at the incompetence of others.
- I can't stand it when things are out of place.
- I find unpredictability vexing if not intolerable.
- I have a burning need to set things right.
- I worry a lot about why I haven't done better.
- Any kind of personal failure is the worst thing I can think of.
- It seems to me that standards are slipping everywhere.

Tap Dancer

- I find it difficult or impossible to tell anyone the whole truth.
- I would rather end a primary relationship than make a binding commitment.

- Figuring out "what I can get away with" is exciting to me.
- I have an abiding fear of being "caught" or "cornered."
- I always have a "Plan B" in mind in case I need to escape.
- To avoid feeling lonely, I have to run faster than I used to.

Remember, no one is perfect. Everyone faces some of these obstacles. Even though we may shake our heads and say, "My God, I'm all of it," the issue is that we can deal with anything we can name. This is not an exercise to see how broken we are, but to understand that if we can identify the obstacles and are willing to work through them, we will increase our ability to "soar like a hawk."

Recap

1. Our own habit patterns prevent us from forming more rewarding relationships.
2. Self-defeating learned behaviors prevent us from getting the "good stuff."

What you live with you learn.
What you learn you practice.
What you practice you become.
What you become has consequences.

Whatever you would make habitual, practice it; and if you would not make a thing habitual, do not practice it, but accustom yourself to something else.

—Epictetus

Who shall guard the guardians themselves?
—Juvenal

Habit with him was all the test of truth;
"It must be right, I've done it since my youth."
—George Crabbe

It matters not how straight the gate,
How charged with punishments the scroll,
I am the master of my fate;
I am the captain of my soul.
—William Ernst Henley

3

HABITS

Understanding the profound effect of habits is critical to Stage II Recovery. Why? Because understanding habits is the essence of understanding change, and there can be no recovery, either Stage I or Stage II, without change.

Most of our lives—what we think, say, do, and become—is the result of habit. And since habits are rooted in our subconscious, they are always active, operating full blast, whether we are aware of them or not. Right now, for good or ill, even as you read this page, your subconscious filter is hard at work sorting all incoming data to fit the form and style of the habits that live there.

A Caretaker, for example, might say, "This is wonderful stuff. *How can I make others use it!*" People-Pleasers may react with quiet desperation: "Oh, God, if I buy this message, I might have to act differently and everyone will get mad at me. If they get mad, I must be bad. If I am bad, they will go away. If they go away, I'll be all alone again. I don't think I like this book." Martyrs may find a curious delight thinking, "This stuff sounds really hard—*Good*. I'm going to *like* this book!"

The fact is that what we live with we learn, what we learn we practice, what we practice we become, and what we become has consequences. There really is no big mystery or secret about what is likely to happen in our lives. If we understand our habits well enough—the habits that constitute our living patterns—there are no surprises. What we rub up against rubs off. It is as simple as that.

Have you ever become aware of a disturbing repetition in your life? Have you ever found yourself, *again*, in a familiar situation that you swore you would avoid forever? Have you wondered why? As you review the track record of your relationships, do you find a certain sameness? Do the same things keep happening to you? Have you ever said in frustrated anger, as a marvelous woman friend recently said to me, "Why is it that every man I like is a jerk?" And did you, as she did, assume the problem to be "all those jerks" rather than her own self-defeating behavior?

The answer to all those questions can be summed up in one word: *Habits.*

Who Is Driving Your Bus?

I once conducted a therapy group on a psych ward. It didn't take me long to realize that this was a marvelous experience that could teach me a great deal if I spent as much time listening and learning as I did directing. One memorable day, a man named Al stole the show. Al's prior experience with drugs was considerable, and as a result he had a terrible time staying in one place. Although his body certainly never left group, his mind came and went constantly. You just never knew when Al would "reappear." On this particular afternoon, he suddenly "showed up" and made this astounding announcement, "I got the answer!" Since no one knew where Al had been, we all paid close attention and, by golly, he *did* have the answer. He said, "Imagine you have a trap door you open up in your forehead. There in your brain is a great big Greyhound steering wheel, a big old leather seat, and even one of those hats with a big badge on it. My problem is I got a junkie driving my bus. The answer is, I got to get the junkie out of my driver's seat."

It doesn't get much clearer than that!

At times we all have a junkie driving our bus. These are the old, bad habits that formed over long periods of time and after an incredible amount of practice. Of course, we weren't aware that we were practicing anything, but we were. People don't "become" anything all of a sudden. We got where we are, for good or ill, after considerable practice and repeated action. And that's not only how we got where we are, but it's precisely how we get somewhere else.

What you are or will be at seventy is what you were at thirty-five—only twice so. How else could it be? Give yourself thirty-five years of intensive practice and you will get very, very good at what you practice. Give your "bus driver" thirty-five, forty, or seventy years to drive the same route hundreds upon hundreds of times a day, and he will be able to do it blindfolded. He will drive the route without even thinking about it. That is exactly what habits do.

Clara is forty-four years old. She married an alcoholic twenty-four years ago. Although she has been in Al-Anon "all my life," as she says, and has certainly gained stability in her life, irritating patterns keep reappearing. She has no idea why, and she often wonders why she married an alcoholic in the first place. Although she "works her program" to the best of her ability, she just doesn't seem to have made much personal progress since dealing with the trauma of an alcoholic marriage some fifteen years ago.

Clara *doesn't know* who is driving her bus. Sure enough, she got a stranglehold on her pain and charged through Stage I Recovery, but it all stopped there. But now, as Clara is taking a long, hard, focused look at her habits, all kinds of lights are going on. Do any of these sound familiar?

- Her mother was a passive martyr who automatically took the blame for any unhappiness, conflict, or problems in her family.
- Her father was an alcoholic who blamed her mother for his problems. Her mother promptly accepted the blame.
- Her "job" as a child was to take care of her brothers and basically not make waves.
- When her father wanted a cup of coffee, he never asked for it, he just banged his cup on the table till

someone got it for him. That "someone" was always Clara or her mother.

• Clara was told a million times that the secret to happiness was "God first, others second, and yourself last."

The list could be much longer. The point is that people like Clara are not stalled *because* they marry alcoholics. Perhaps it is because they were stalled *that* they married alcholics. Since our living problems are mostly a matter of habits, attacking them is first a matter of understanding that what you lived with, you practiced, and what you practiced, you became. It is no mystery that the same irritating consequences keep coming up in Clara's life. She is good at what she has practiced. Habits create consequences.

Principles

Spend a few minutes now reflecting on these principles of habits:

1. *As much as 98 percent of what we do is the result of habit, not choice.* Acting out habits is not a matter of choice because habits operate outside of the conscious mind, where choices are made.

   Of course, not all habits are bad habits. Our very best traits are also habits—self-enhancing habits—and they become habits the same way our self-defeating habits become part of us: by practice. The beneficial habits we can just leave alone. Let them operate making good things appear in our lives. We need to concern ourselves with the self-defeating habits, which keep us from enjoying all that life has to offer.

   It is incredible to realize that as we merrily go about our day—responding, reacting, thinking, feeling, doing—we aren't making real decisions about what we are doing. "The junkie in the driver's seat" simply takes the wheel and drives off. With our lives.

Recovery is the willingness to put up that fight and to refuse the driver's seat to hijacker habits.

2. *Whatever we do consistently will become a habit.* To a large extent, we don't choose our habits. Or at least we *didn't.* Clara, as a small girl, wasn't aware that she was creating habits by acting out what she was taught. Children, of course, don't discern what is healthy and what is not. They simply strive in the best way they know to get the love and acceptance that is necessary to all human beings.

What we practice, we become.

Men who don't share feelings most often aren't holding back out of pure wickedness and spite. They *don't know how* to share their feelings because they have never practiced sharing them. What they did practice was to "get tough." Consistently—in what they thought, did, and felt—they brought about the truth that "real men don't." Rather than say, "I hurt," many men would rather bleed to death right in front of the women who would sell their souls to be let in.

3. *What we practice we become good at.* And if we have a natural talent on top of all that practice, we become not only good but world-class! World-class People-Pleasers, for example, will apologize profoundly for asking you to get off their foot while tears of pain roll down their cheeks. It's no act. They actually *think* they have no right to inconvenience you. They *feel* great sorrow and guilt at inconveniencing you. They *act* out their passive thoughts and feelings as long as they possibly can. Only when the pain gets too great are they forced to timidly, regretfully ask you to *please* get off their crushed foot!

How did they, the world-class Caretakers, Workaholics, Perfectionists get so darn good? How did Peter, a friend of mine, get to be such a skillful Perfectionist? When Peter mows his lawn he carries a ruler on his tractor so he can periodically jump off to make sure the grass is exactly three inches high. Peter is now working on his third marriage. Until he got into Stage II Recovery, he would seriously ask me, "Say, what is wrong with women anyway? Why did my first two wives never want to help me?" His present marriage has a chance of working because now he is not asking questions about "them" but looking at himself and the habits that run his bus without his knowledge or permission. How do we get so good? The same way we get good at anything—we take lessons and then we practice. Hard.

4. *Habits are living things. Whatever is alive will fight to the death to stay alive.* Most of us don't realize this about habits. When we practice a habit, we give it life. That habit exists independently in our subconscious and it is going to defend its space there and fight to stay alive, just as all living things do. Initiating a new habit is a real battle. Picture, if you will, the old habit as a king sitting on his throne. You are a general creating a new army to dethrone him. Do you think that king is going to be happy to see you coming down the road? Of course not. King Habit is going to do everything possible to defeat you. Advance guards—feelings of fear, guilt, and anger—will be sent out to make you back down and run away. No king gives up easily. But if we accept the fact that change is a battle, the challenge becomes pretty clear cut: a powerful king is on the throne and wants to stay there. But the fact is that if we allow our feelings to dictate our actions, *we will never mount an attack that can give anything else power.*

Recovery is nothing short of civil war. It demands that we literally go to war with ourselves, specifically with our own habits. Those people who don't understand the role and depth of habits set themselves up to fail in recovery because they underestimate the magnitude of the task.

5. *Frustration is always relative to expectations.* If we have unrealistic expectations, we quickly become frustrated. Nothing is more deeply rooted in us than our habits. Nothing is more "who we are" than our habits. Even if our habits result in painful consequences, they are *familiar*, comfortable consequences. The challenges of striving to establish something different and new for ourselves, based on a new vision, a new quest, or a new set of rules is truly the striving of heroes.

Recovery is a civil war that is worth fighting, because victory brings personal growth and freedom —specifically, the freedom to become ever more capable of functioning in loving relationships.

Making It Personal

Again, with paper and pencil at hand, fill in the blank: "According to my best insight, the habit pattern I most need to change, because it's limiting my recovery, is this:

_____."

Perhaps you put down something like these answers:

• Not asking for what I need.
• Allowing others to dictate my feelings.
• Demanding that others make me happy.
• Worrying.
• Procrastinating.
• Being a Perfectionist.
• Forcing situations to get my way.
• Feeling that only a man/woman relationship can give me self-worth.
• Automatically assuming that others know more than I know.

What Habits Do

Now that you have made a personal statement about your task during Stage II Recovery, let's work with that habit more specifically. Habits have three functions, which means that the specific habit *you* declared has three functions.

Habits Act as Thermostats

The fundamental difference between thermostats and thermometers has often been noted. Thermostats control the environment. Thermometers merely record it. Our habits are our personal "reality thermostats"— they ensure that the environment stays comfortable by compelling us to act exactly the way we see ourselves. Each of our habits, operating without our awareness, has its own "thermostat" that is regulated to protect what is "normal." Anytime we contemplate or carry out differing thoughts, feelings, or actions, our thermostats fly into operation.

Let's say that the habit pattern you wrote down was something like this: "I have a great deal of difficulty allowing myself to have a good time or even admitting that I am having a good time. I am a 'Martyr.'"

Whenever you think or actually behave unlike a Martyr, your thermostat will go crazy. You may get sick. (Headaches are effective at ruining a good time.) "All of a sudden" you may be hit with a terrible avalanche of self-criticism. "For no reason" you may be flooded with visions of all the starving children in the world. Then emotional withdrawal takes place, and you find yourself in one of those terrible clipped conversations:

"How are you doing?" "Fine."

"Isn't this a nice day?" "Yeah."

"Aren't we going to have fun today!" "Maybe."

Similarly, the Workaholic "all of a sudden" has a fit of the "guilts" when contemplating time off; the People-Pleaser inexplicably becomes nauseated; the Tap Dancer finally makes the decision to end a relationship because the other person is too tall, or too fat, or left-handed (when actually he or she was just too honest).

Our personal thermostats are as ingenious and powerful as our deepest selves, for that is the source of their power. The function of this subconscious self, which some call "the robot" and some liken to the program fed into a computer, is merely to *defend*. I call this thermostat the "Guardian," since its sole role is to judge, assess, or make value judgments about this being healthy or not—merely to defend.

Here's a story that may help explain. My sister owns a lovable fifteen-year-old mutt dog named Tiger. Tiger is one of those dogs that's as much a part of the family as any human member—and he knows it. Recently, little old Tiger got into a terrible fight with a German Shepherd that had made the unforgivable mistake of wandering into Tiger's yard. Since Tiger has lost most of his teeth, the best he could hope to do was maybe gum the Shepherd to death. Not surprisingly, Tiger took such a brutal thrashing that we feared that he had eaten his last dog biscuit.

I asked my sister why Tiger would charge a dog so much larger and stronger. Her answer was simply, "Oh, Earnie, Tiger doesn't know size. Tiger only knows defend." That is how the Guardian is. It makes no distinction; it merely defends with all its ingenuity and might.

Consider *your* Guardian. When you even *think* about ousting your target habit from power, how does your Guardian react? What responses do you experience?

1. _____
2. _____
3. _____

Habits Defend Reality

The second function of habits has to do with our feelings—our habits' first line of defense. They are like the
attack dogs that King Habit unleashes when he sees an
enemy approaching.

The important thing to know is that feelings only face
backwards; they only know what *was*. We have sent our
feelings to school a million times. We have learned
which behaviors make us feel normal and which do not.

That is why feelings cannot be our guide to a new way
of life. If we, as most people do, allow our feelings to be
the sole dictator of how we act, then obviously there will
be no lasting new behavior. And if nothing changes,
nothing changes.

I'm not saying that feelings are bad or the enemy, and
I'm certainly not saying that we should not be in touch
with how we feel. Knowing how we feel, in fact, is
critical in our journey into Stage II Recovery. But it is
just as important that we do not allow how we feel to be
the only factor that determines how we act.

The truth is that *if you want to change how you feel, you
must change how you act and keep at it long enough until
acting in a healthy manner is as comfortable as acting in a
self-defeating manner used to be.*

The task is formidable. A fairly good definition of
insanity might be to expect different results from the
same behavior. Different results don't come from the
same old behavior. Different results can only come
from *different* behavior. And the obstacle to consistent,
new behavior is almost always feelings.

The first time People-Pleasers decide to say, "No!
This is my right and I will not tolerate being short-
changed," how do they feel? *Panic* is too tame a word.
There may well be *no* adequate word. They worry, feel
tormented, sweat; they may get headaches and diar-
rhea. Their knees will knock and their Guardian will

generate countless reasons and ways to stop this foolishness and get back to what is normal. If People-Pleasers allow feelings to dictate their behavior, will they ever say no? No.

Suppose your subconscious self says, "Who are you kidding? You weren't meant to be a success. You will never make this big sale." So you march against King Habit and throw down the challenge, affirming, "I *am* capable. I deserve to reach the top. I *will* make the sale." How might you feel? What might your Guardian do?

Until you affirm and "act successful" long enough, until it becomes as much a part of who you are as the opposite was before, you will probably feel like a bowl of Jello. Your Guardian will fight to make you "accidentally late" for the important meeting. "Somehow" you won't notice the catsup stain on your tie. You "just won't believe" the incredible blunder you made when you were talking with the prospective client.

Expect mood swings when you start to engage your living patterns in civil war. After all, you are on new, frightening, hotly contested grounds. Your feelings don't really care what behavior they bind to. They only ask you to act consistently enough so they know what behavior generates the "this-is-comfortable" button, and what behavior triggers the "this-feels-awful" response.

The following illustrations have made sense to many of my clients:

GUARANTEED STUCK IN THE PAST

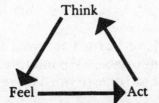

NECESSARY FOR RECOVERY

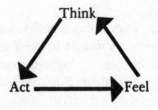

Again—consider your specific habit-in-need-of-change. How do you feel when you plan or begin to act against your long-practiced, firmly established habits? *Know your feelings:*

1. _____
2. _____
3. _____

The question is, who shall decide? Will you allow what you *know* to be sane, healthy behavior to begin to take root in your subconscious so that your Guardian will automatically defend what is to your benefit? Or, faithful to the past model, will you be unwilling to fight your way through the temporary difficulty of unpleasant feelings? If so, you will allow feelings to dictate behavior and never journey far into Stage II Recovery. And the journey you do make will be heavy with consequences.

If we are going to change, we have to let what we *know* dictate how we act. An unrecognized, unexamined, unacceptable feeling is a madman in the driver's seat. And if we don't take a good hard look at that fact, at the habit system that's in place, we don't have a chance at changing.

Most of us have learned to avoid any feeling that makes us uncomfortable. We interpret an uncomfortable feeling as a bad one, so when we're uncomfortable, we usually stop the behavior that is making us feel that way. *And this is exactly why most people do not continue in programs of change.* New behavior has to swim upstream against entrenched feelings. We are going to be uncomfortable because doing something new feels different. We have to learn that it's OK to feel uncomfortable for a while. We have to expect it and accept it.

When we decide to let what we *know* (rather than what we *feel*) dictate what we *do*, we are ready to formulate a program of change that will work. If you are someone, for example, who withdraws at parties, someone who is not even willing to go out and talk to people because you're in the habit of saying, "They're all idiots, they have nothing to say to me and I have nothing to say to them," then you're quite skilled at thinking of a million reasons why you shouldn't go anywhere because you don't want to feel uncomfortable. Be prepared to feel uncomfortable the first time you go to a party. So what? It doesn't make any difference. You may be shaking in your shoes, but if you *expect* that feeling, you will be able to control it. *Frustration is always relative to expectation.*

Habits Define What Is Normal

Habits function in a third way. They act like emotional glasses that we wear from morning to night. It is through those glasses that we view, interpret, and evaluate our reality. None of us really sees reality the way *it* is. We see reality the way *we* are.

To a Martyr, for example, all of reality is an accident waiting to happen to them. The world is full of disappointments and incompetence. This is true about the world, but this is all the Martyr sees. It is *the* truth. Dreadful things are "normal."

People-Pleasers find it normal to hide and have fearful expectation of others' "getting mad" and going away. They expect it, so their Guardian does its best to comply. What we think about, we talk about. What we talk about, we bring about. It is "just normal."

Specifically, the question is, "What is normal for you?" Every time I ask a certain friend of mine, "How is it going?" he says, "Life is a struggle." For him, it is and will always be until he is willing to go to war with that habit or way of looking at reality.

This particular friend has been sober for nearly fifteen years. He has almost memorized the Big Book. He attends countless meetings and has sponsored dozens and dozens of others in the Twelve Step program. He has yet to find much happiness. When his wife left him (for many reasons, only one of which was, "I just can't stand that negative frame of mind"), he wasn't surprised. He expected it. *Life is a struggle.* He knew it would happen. It did happen. It was normal.

Three Outs

If we are not on guard when new data conflicts with old habits, we tend to opt for these "outs":

1. *We invalidate the information.* Have you ever done this? After hearing or reading something that challenges old habits, the tendency is to think, "This is ridiculous stuff. Who would ever believe that? It can't be done."

2. *We invalidate the source.* We simply negate it all by saying, "The guy is a jerk. What does he know? If he were walking in my shoes, he wouldn't say such a stupid thing." That justifies staying stuck.

3. *We remove ourselves from the source of the conflicting data.* That is, if you happen on a meeting where you encounter conflicting data, the tendency is to say, "See if I ever go back to that group. Not one of them has his head on straight."

The Guardian is subtle and strong. Take a little time with a pencil and paper and jot down your own examples. When have you given in to any of the three "outs" when King Habit got his toes stepped on?

Recap

1. Whatever we practice becomes a habit.
2. Habits are rooted in our subconscious, where they function without our awareness or our permission.
3. Since habits are alive, they will, like anything living, fight to stay alive.
4. We have *learned* to feel certain ways.

*There is nothing more dangerous
than ignorance in action.*

They can because they think they can.
—Virgil

The future is purchased by the present.
—Samuel Johnson

*Those who cannot remember the past are condemned to repeat
it.*
—George Santayana

4

CHANGE

Recovery *is* and *demands* change. Recovery means that
things have to be different than they were. It means
that *I* have to be different than I was. All change is
about changing habits, which is why a basic understanding of habits is essential to understanding, and ultimately initiating, change.

Stage I Recovery is certainly all about change. Look
at the difference between being drunk and being sober;
between secretly, compulsively overeating and control-
ling that compulsion; between engaging in compulsive
sexual behavior and refraining from that behavior.
Dramatic, heroic, marvelous change is clearly evident.

The changes in Stage II Recovery are equally dramatic, however. Observe the difference between never saying no and being able to stand up for yourself; between somehow always ending up in destructive relationships and being able to make a choice; between never finding any fault with yourself and being willing to take responsibility for your own consequences.

One of the greatest joys of my life was when two new parents, carrying their six-month-old son, approached me one day at church. They held him out, saying, "The cycle stops here." Both parents had attended several of my workshops and seminars; both had begun truly walking the road of Stage II Recovery, and so they had a precious gift of freedom to offer their new son. We all get what we are willing to pay for.

Change—all change—takes place in three sequential steps:
1. Conversion
2. Decision
3. Action

In this chapter, we will cover the first two steps, conversion and decision. Chapter 5 will deal with action, the third step.

Conversion

In my experience, we do not change *until we have some kind of awakening to the fact that we are going to lose something we are not prepared to live without if we do not change.* I call that awakening a conversion experience. Some people call it "hitting the wall" or "kissing concrete." No matter what it's called, the experience is the same. Until we have it, we simply don't see the ultimate destination of the path we have been traveling (which is the result of the habits we have been practicing). Until that

turning point comes, we just don't have the where-
withal, the get-up-and-go, the strength, the motivation
to do the things that make change start.

The term "hitting the wall" is used by runners who
say that in a marathon, usually around the twentieth
mile, going on is like smashing into a concrete wall.
From that point on, they say, you discover what you are
made of. You also hit that psychological wall as part of
the process of change—the moment at which you know
that if you don't change, if something really different
doesn't get going, then you are going to lose something
you're not prepared to live without.

Until there is a conversion experience, what is in
control of our lives? What filters all incoming data and
reshapes it to fit our notion of what is normal?

Sure—habits.

A conversion experience happens when we "hit the
wall" hard enough that our perceptions are altered.
Due to the impact of the collision, maybe just momentarily, we see a different possibility than those automatically offered up by our prevailing habits. As you can see
by now, that usually takes a considerable wallop.

Some people's conversion experiences are accompa-
nied by lights and whistles. Others' experiences are as
quiet and simple as an evening breeze. But the core of
the experience is that *enough is enough*. We simply see a
new light or an old light with new eyes. In all of my
years of working a program and counseling, nothing has
ever come close to the amazement I feel when I see this
conversion experience in people. Words really don't fit
this mystery. The fact simply is that when it's your time,
it's your time.

A working definition might well be this: "A conversion experience happens when a person accepts—which
is far deeper than just knowing—that if I do not change
I will lose something or someone I am not prepared to
live without."

As the thinking goes, "If you are prepared to lose it, you will." How much do you have to lose before you "kiss concrete"? That is the mystery. Who knows? But at some point you *will* know that this is different. This is enough.

Wall-butting may occur when a person

- hears a spouse say, "It's over";
- watches a successful, middle-aged friend die of a sudden heart attack and realizes, "My life is not forever";
- has thought once too often and seriously about how lovely and easy it would be to end it all;
- realizes she has hit her child too hard—too often;
- sees through "peace by acquisition" and accepts that it will never bring the fulfillment that owning things seems to promise;
- looks in a mirror and says, "I hate you";
- hears a doctor say, "Mend your ways or you'll never see another Christmas";
- sees tears in the eyes of a loved one and finally accepts responsibility for that pain;
- hears the whistle blow at quitting time and knows he is trapped forever in a nowhere place and job;
- starts to cry himself to sleep again and realizes that no one cares; or
- has failed for the umpteenth time and suddenly realizes that she has caused that failure because she didn't believe she could ever really win.

I could give examples for any habit. The point is that each of us has to identify for ourselves what we are going to lose if we don't change the habit we wrote down. Why *should* I change? That's the question. What am I going to lose if I don't? What can I hang onto, or gain, if I do? So often the ready response is, "Oh, but it's going to hurt so much, it's going to be so difficult." And if you are saying those kinds of things as you contemplate change, the chances are good that you haven't hit the wall, yet.

When you've smacked up against the wall, what is to be lost is so great that *it doesn't make any difference* how much it takes to make the gain or stop the loss. The real and certain imminence of the loss is so overpowering that *the cost just doesn't matter.*

Another example: Let's say that you are driving along and you see that a car has veered off the road and tumbled down a hill, where it's on fire and in danger of blowing up. You're standing on top of the hill looking down and, of course, you are concerned, but you know that if you ran down there and tried to pull the people out of the wreckage, you might blow up along with them. But as you look closer, you see that the car looks kind of familiar. In an instant you realize that it's one of your cars and that the people trapped down there are not just people—they're your children. What do you do? All of a sudden you realize that if you don't go down there and do something, you're going to lose something you're not prepared to live without. Like a flash you are down that hill.

What do you think about as you run? Are you thinking of the negative things that may happen? Are you concerned that your clothes will get ripped and muddy? Of course not. What you have to gain by going down there and saving the lives of your kids is so great that nothing else matters.

A curious and mysterious phenomenon comes in to play here. It's amazing how much people are prepared to lose before they are willing to do anything to effect change. *How much are you prepared to lose?* is an extremely important question. How much pain are you prepared to feel before you are ready to do something that can really make change happen?

I know I will never forget a client I had many years ago, a lovely woman I had seen many times and had become very fond of. One day she came in about ten o'clock in the morning wearing sunglasses. As we sat and talked, she told me about a violent confrontation between her and the alcoholic she was living with. As she sat there telling me that he had tried to shoot her, I found it incredible that she could tell the story with such resignation—as if they had had words over an unpaid bill or a poorly prepared meal. When I started to talk about changing things, she said, "I am used to living there. It's so hard to change. Where would I go?" How much was she prepared to lose?

Finally she took off her sunglasses and I saw that her eyes were beaten and bruised. She continued to say that change was hard, and I continued to ask her how hard it was to live as she was living. She simply was not willing to make a change.

Relative to the habit you identified earlier, how much are you prepared to lose? Or, are you prepared to pay that price to let that habit stay in control? If the answer is yes, then change will never happen, no matter how much insight you get from books or lectures or tapes or your group or program. Why? Because you simply don't have enough reason or motivation to change. What you are going to lose isn't that bad. What you are going to gain by staying there is acceptable. If what you are going to lose isn't real, personal, and deeply perceived, the change process just can't get rolling.

The Second First Step

Everyone familiar with the Twelve Step program knows that the First Step is called the desperation step. You take it when enough is enough, when things get to such a point that you say, "I don't care what it takes. I'll do anything. Anything. But I am not willing to continue this way."

Until there is a First Step, there is nothing
Stage II Recovery takes another First Step. We call it the Second First Step. With it, you become as serious

about your living patterns and habits as you were about the addiction that brought you into the program in the first place. Until the Second First Step happens, there is no Stage II Recovery.

In the past dozen or so years, I have increasingly noticed, especially in working with recovering alcoholics, that somewhere between two and six years of sobriety, when they think they have climbed the toughest mountain and put all the hard stuff behind them, they come nose-crunching up against the real mountain: themselves and their self-defeating learned behaviors. And more often than not, relationship problems led them to realize that they needed some kind of continued growth. As one friend put it, "I just can't get my relationships on the dance floor. Most often I can't even get near the music."

Conversion is certainly a tricky word. Some people get it quite confused with a dramatic religious experience. Some think of it only in terms of a blinding flash of light and a voice from the void. These may indeed be conversion experiences, but not all conversion experiences are like these.

A conversion experience simply means that you've come to the point where enough is enough. It is when you turn a corner in your emotional/spiritual/psychological life and say, "No more." From there on, no matter what it takes, things will be different.

Let's take a look at some principles and facts about conversion experiences.

Spiritual Reality

Conversion experiences are spiritual realities. By that, I do not mean that they are religious, but spiritual in the sense that they aren't rooted in reason. There is something deeper going on than just the rational, "does-this-make-sense?" approach. Sure it makes sense and is smart to stop drinking, or stop smoking, or stop seeing this person who continually cuts you down. It makes all the sense in the world. But that doesn't mean that all the sense known to God or man necessarily *makes any difference.* So what does and when? When it is time, it is time.

The reason for understanding the spiritual dimension of conversion is to help you be patient and kind to yourself. Beating yourself up because you aren't ready to truly effect change is a lose-lose situation. The more you put yourself down, the less you believe that you deserve the good things that come with change. So you stay stuck.

The most you can do to "cause" a conversion experience is to create a state of readiness. *Work* at becoming ready. Invite the light. Be prepared so that when it comes, you won't be inside with the doors locked.

Changes vs. Change

There is a vast difference between changes and change. Making some changes means that you are merely doing the same old thing in a different way. Same play, new stage. Change means doing something that is really different—so different that it can't be accomplished without breaking through the old patterns. If there is no war with the Guardian, chances are you are not involved with change.

In an effort to avoid going to war with ourselves, we tend to attempt changes rather than change in the recovery effort. A male-dependent woman, for example, will keep away from a certain bar where she has met many men before, but she keeps operating in the same pattern with men she meets at church. Or a person, in the name of recovery, stops drinking Scotch and switches to beer. Or someone may make a dramatic commitment to stop binge-eating. She absolutely leaves hot fudge alone—and now only stockpiles chocolate chip cookies.

If there is to be genuine change, what must people do who have trouble buying anything for themselves? Only one thing. They must start buying gifts for themselves. The problem is the Guardian, of course. But the only way out is *through*.

People-Pleasers must start to say no even though they would rather walk barefoot to the North Pole. But there is only one way to break old habits, which is at the core of change: *do what you are afraid to do*. Face the Guardian down, nose to nose.

The Tap Dancer needs to stand still and say, "Here I am. All of me. No hustle, no half-truth, no back door escapes. This is me and here I make a commitment."

Sure, the very thought is enough to make us howl in agony. But change, doing something truly different, is the only way old patterns are overturned.

Changing Others

Have you ever attempted to change others? Has it worked? Of course not. No one can change another person. Why? Because the First Step of change is conversion and no one can have another person's conversion experience. Even though you *know* you are right. Even though you are so *sure* that what you see as truth *is* the truth. Even though you are watching someone you dearly love self-destruct right before your very eyes— still, with all the anguish and hurt that goes along with it, *you cannot have anyone else's conversion experience*.

If a person is young enough, can you make him go to church? Sure. Can you make him have a personal relationship with his Higher Power? No. Can you force someone into treatment? Sure. Can you force someone to cheerfully embrace sobriety? No. Can you force someone who has achieved Stage I Recovery into embarking on the path of Stage II Recovery? Absolutely not.

Understanding and accepting this fact can go a long way toward preventing a broken heart. If you are taking on the responsibility for another's conversion experience, you are guaranteed no end of frustration and suffering.

Enabling

Once a person understands that conversion is initiated by a sense of loss and pain, the real harm "enablers" do in the name of love becomes clear. By definition, enablers are those who shield others from the consequences of their own irresponsible behavior. If you are that buffer, then your loved one will never feel the very pain that alone can bring him to a spiritual conversion experience.

Sometimes, with the very best of intentions and in the name of the truest love, we grossly hinder a loved one's chances for a better life. How? By enabling. We smother their chance.

Systems

The last principle of the conversion experience, which is the First Step of change, involves a preliminary understanding of the systems of relationships. None of us lives in a vacuum. We all live in networks of relationships that I call systems. Imagine a spiderweb. When one spider on a strand of that web begins to move, the whole web is set in motion. Our own networks of relationships are just as sensitive as that spiderweb. Any movement or change by one person affects the whole network.

The point is that just because you have had a conversion experience and are ready to change, don't assume that everyone else (or anyone else) in your system has had a similar experience and is also anxious to change.

This disparity confuses many newly recovering persons. What is needed and why it is needed is so clear to them that their new paths spread out before them in absolute brilliance. But then, all too often, they find that those closest to them do not support and are sometimes downright hostile to their new efforts.

Expect it to happen. Because *you* decide not to be a Caretaker, does that mean that the babies you have trained all those years suddenly don't want to be babies anymore? Because you are willing, at great cost to yourself, to go to war with the Guardian of your People-Pleasing patterns, does that mean those you have said yes to all those years are going to be thrilled at your new no? Of course not.

Imagine one of those old vest-pocket watches. Open the back of the watch and see the amazing machinery. Wheels, sprockets, springs—all whirring and clicking together. Now imagine that this amazing complexity is all bent out of shape. The wheels are not round, the springs are sprung, and the sprockets no longer fit right. But because they are *all* out of shape, somehow they click along, still working. Now take out one of those dented wheels. Fix it. Make it truly round so that all the spokes are in place. Shine it up. Fine. It looks great—but where are you going to put it? Even though that part has been repaired, none of the other parts have changed. The fixed part doesn't fit.

Decision

Decision is the Second Step of change. A conversion experience not followed by a decision is a wasted miracle. Instead of changing, a new life that could have produced truly different results was allowed to flicker and die, locked in the bondage of old habits. So, once again (1) think of the habit that you will go to war with to progress along the path of your Stage II Recovery, (2) fix firmly in your mind what you will lose if you don't, and (3) look now at the qualities of a valid decision.

It Must Be Your Decision

Just as no one can have your conversion experience, no one can make your decision for you. A conversion experience is the launching pad for a genuine decision and nothing less. If someone else decides you should make a decision, you won't "hit the wall" hard enough to alter your perceptions. We can only change for ourselves, and we only change when the consequences of acting out that habit or that pattern have become so painful that we are no longer willing to pay the price. When we realize that, a conversion experience will follow and we can make a decision that is our own. In addition to being your *own*, a decision must be wholehearted. Nothing is held back in a valid decision.

All too often, when we think about making decisions, we fall into the trap of figuring out what we are willing to do to make the change happen. But it is not what we are willing to do that makes the difference. The difference is, *what does it take?* A person may say, "I am willing to change by reading books, going to seminars, and even filling out some of these lines; but I am not willing to go to group. And I am surely not willing to talk to anybody else about what's wrong." That kind of decision is not going to make it. *It is not our willingness to do something that makes the difference; it is our willingness to do what it takes.*

Say that someone has discovered that a major obstacle to his Stage II Recovery is his inability to share feelings, caused perhaps by an inability to get in touch with them. He may then say, "Here's what I am willing to do! I am willing to write about it. I am willing to think about it. I am willing to pray about it. But I am not willing to go to my wife and tell her that I love her. I am not willing to tell my kids what makes me angry." This person is really saying that he is not willing to actually do what it takes.

Some counseling sessions are almost a comedy routine. A client will say, "Look, I really want to get over being a People-Pleaser. I honestly do. There is nothing in the world that causes me more pain, and I am *committed* to working on it." I say, "OK, then what this is going to take is this: with your support group, you are going to have to learn to say no." And the client says, "Oh, no, I can't do that! Let's sit here in your office and talk about it. Let's plan how we can get around this. Tell me what books to read." And my answer always is, "Well, certainly we can do things like that, but the bottom line is that you are going to have to learn to say no." The client says, "You don't understand. I just can't do that. I'm not willing to go that far right now, but I really want to get over it." And so it may go for hour after hour. The bottom line and the inescapable fact is that change is never a matter of picking and choosing what you are willing to do. Once the conversion experience has happened, the issue comes down to this basic question: *What is it going to take to make this change happen?* And the answer is the only thing that will really make a difference.

So get your paper and pencil and think about what it is going to take for *you* to break the habit that you have written down as your obstacle.

Every Yes Is Also a No

In making and talking about decisions, we sometimes tend to think that saying yes is the easy part. But every yes requires a no. If, for example, we say yes to sobriety, then we also have to say no to hanging around certain old friends. If we say yes to overcoming eating binges, then we must learn to say no to hanging out at donut and pie shops. Every yes is also a no, but sometimes the yes is far easier than the no.

The point is, if we are going to march steadily down a new road, we have to keep away from slippery people and slippery places. It is imperative as we look at change and at the quality of our decisions, that we know what *our* slippery people and slippery places are. Changing our living patterns to avoid slippery people and slippery places often means giving up certain events, people, and entertainment that we have become very comfortable with. That's difficult. But saying no is really important.

Why does every yes require a no? Because changing habits is central to Stage II Recovery. Every time we allow ourselves to be around the old people and places, we are giving the old habit power again. Changing habits and changing patterns must always move toward the new. It is obviously very important to keep away from those people and places that tend to generate the old stimuli, the old feelings, and the old responses.

As you look at the habit that gets in the way of your Stage II Recovery, think carefully about what you are going to have to say yes and no to?

Every Time Counts

Sometimes we slack off once we have successfully accomplished *one behavior* that is contrary to the Guardian. The first time that a Martyr relaxes and allows herself to have a good time, or the first time a Workaholic stops working and takes some time off really feels good. You may get so excited and so happy about that a little victory that you say, "Well, I've got that habit beat!" But, of course, it isn't true!

Once is not enough. A conversion experience is like putting a match to gunpowder. The big burst of initial power that really gets you off the launching pad may make you feel that you are totally beyond it. But habits die hard, and whatever is alive fights to the death to stay alive. To let down your guard, to think that you have it beat, is to delude yourself. As soon as the light and the heat of the conversion experience is past, it is all too easy, six months down the road, to find yourself right back where you started.

A crucial quality of a valid decision is the clear-eyed realization that once is not enough. You have to act against your habit over and over and over again. Since you didn't become *who you are* by practicing those behaviors once, you are going to have to keep at it again and again and again. Once is not enough and every time counts. I am not saying that you should become a Perfectionist and lean so hard on yourself that every time you slip and find yourself back in an old pattern, you should declare your recovery ruined and kick yourself for not making better progress. Be very patient and kind with yourself. But if you choose to go back to the old ways, don't tell yourself that it doesn't make a difference. Every time *does* count. You need to understand how important a truth that is.

Keep Your Eye on the Goal

Change is civil war. Recovery centers on change. If we are not willing to go to war with ourselves, we will not have the success we want in Stage II Recovery. When things get hard, it is vitally important that we keep our sights on the goal. We have made a difficult decision to put up this fight. We are clear about why we have to keep going, because we understand what we are going to lose if we don't. *Don't lose sight of your goal.*

All too often in the fight, we feel so overwhelmed with how hard it is and with the struggle to overcome our old habits that we don't focus on the favor that we are doing ourselves. What are we going to gain? And, in fact, what are we gaining every day as we move along? It is important to spend time thinking about this. It is important enough that we might keep a daily log of the progress we have made. Every day we should call to mind *the reason* why we are willing to go to war with these old habits. *Keep your eye on the goal.*

Celebrate All Success

Celebrating all success is an antidote to our tendency to look ahead and see how far we have to go, rather than to look backwards and see how far we have come. When we don't give ourselves credit for how far we have come, we devalue the journey. The more we devalue ourselves, by telling ourselves that we really aren't making much progress, the more our self-image is damaged. And the more we damage our self-image and self-respect, the less reason we have for making a change. But our reason for making changes in the first place was that we deserve better! Or at least that we are not willing to suffer the same kind of pain. So it is important to be patient. It is important to be kind. It is important to celebrate every success we have along the way of change.

Map out for yourself the kind of celebration you could give yourself for all of the work you're doing. A celebration does not always require food and it does not have to be eccentric. Many of us really celebrate when we give ourselves a little *time.* Do *you* have enough time to do things you like, that are enjoyable, that make a difference to you?

We *need* to celebrate. If all we do is look backward and see how strong those old habits are and how painful the struggle is, we won't be motivated to make progress. Celebration is not a luxury.

A conversion experience, when it's followed by a true decision, changes things. Life will not be the same. Why? Because now we see a new light or an old light in a new way. In the next chapter, we will take a look at putting the desire to change and the insight of the conversion experience into a concrete practical program of change.

Recap

1. Recovery is and demands change.
2. Change takes place in three steps: conversion, decision, and action.
3. A conversion experience awakens us to the fact that we are going to lose something we are not prepared to live without if we do not change.
4. A decision involves our willingness to do *what it takes* (not just do *something*) to change.

A journey of a thousand miles must begin with a single step.
                                                    —Lao Tzu

Practice is the best of all instructors.
                                                    —Publilius Syrus

First say to yourself what you would be; and then do what you have to do.

                                                    —Epictetus

The longest journey is the journey inwards of him who has chosen his destiny, who has started his quest for the source of his being.

                                                    —Dag Hammarskjold

5

WORKING A PROGRAM

If you had to make a long trip, what kind of vehicle would you be looking for? Would you have much confidence in a car with bald tires and a leaky radiator? Would you set out on the first day without knowing whether your car had any oil in it? Of course not. You'd check the car first to make sure it was capable of taking you where you wanted to go. No one wants to risk a long trip in a car that doesn't meet certain operational criteria. Why? Because the trip would be delayed and miserable, or you might not get to your destination at all.

The same goes for your program. If you want your program to *work*—to *take* you somewhere—you need to check it out regularly to see that it meets minimal operational standards. Just as you wouldn't trust sheepskin seat covers or a fancy hood ornament to take you from Chicago to Nashville, don't deceive yourself that a program that is merely comfortable and showy is actually going to move you along. Any program of power and substance needs to meet certain criteria.

An Effective Program

The four characteristics of an effective program are these: It must be *concrete*, *practical*, *focused*, and *consistent*.

Concrete and Practical

A program that is vague and nebulous isn't going to get you very far. You have to nail it down. Why? Let's say that you are just starting out in a typing class. Right now, you don't know how to type—you don't have that skill. Suppose the teacher comes in and says, "What do you want to do tonight? Shall we play cards? Or do you want to talk about the ball game?" Are you going to advance your typing skills in that class? Obviously not. But suppose the teacher says, "Turn to page six. Start practicing the sentences there and I'll circulate around the room to see how you're doing." Will that approach advance your typing skills? Most certainly.

We don't change from unskilled to skilled by fooling around. We form all new behavioral patterns by repeated action. Practical and concrete acts, practiced faithfully, nail down the new tracks that lead in the new direction.

Focused

Focus means exactly that. A generalized orientation just doesn't work. If the dentist asked you which tooth hurt, you wouldn't tell him to drill them all. Or if the mechanic can't figure out what's wrong with your car, there isn't much chance that he can fix it, is there? You want to be very specific about *what* you want to change so you can focus on it.

Over the years I have worked with hundreds and hundreds of people who thought they were working a good program. But if you asked them exactly *what* they were trying to change—they didn't know. The specific habit, behavior, and feeling needs to be identified. What are *you* focusing on? What exactly is it that you want to change? If you can't answer that question, your program can't be very useful as a means of change.

When I think of focus I always think of the prize I liked best in a box of Cracker Jacks when I was a child— a little magnifying glass. I liked to make a little pile of leaves, hold the magnifying glass to catch the sun, and try to focus enough solar power on the leaves to start a fire. That's what a program is: a magnifying glass that focuses the power of your program on a habit or behavior that needs to be changed. Without focus, a program can't do that.

Consistent

An effective program also has to be consistent. Since habits are formed by repeated actions, we need to continue the new behavior until it becomes strong enough to have a life of its own. Practiced consistently, that new habit will become who we are. Practiced inconsistently, it won't have a chance. Remember that many of us don't get far with our programs because new behavior makes us uncomfortable, and we've been trained to believe that anything that *feels* uncomfortable must be wrong for us. If we don't understand what's going on, we will stop the new behavior because it doesn't feel comfortable. If we don't practice the new habit over and over, we can't keep it operative, so the old habit stays in control.

Concrete, practical, focused, consistent. Those are the characteristics of a program that can take you somewhere.

Putting a Program Together

What is *your* pile of leaves? That is, what habit or behavioral pattern most stands in the way between you and the better, freer life you would like to have? Before I started to work this out for myself, I really had no idea where my program should be focused. I was so out of touch with what my habits and motives were that I simply couldn't answer that question. Finally, after a great deal of work, I hit on four main behavioral patterns that were causing me no end of trouble and self-defeat.

If you are willing to work to put a program together, you too will get clearer about what you need to deal with. If it's worth it to you and if there is something you're not prepared to lose, you will find your focus.

The four main patterns or character traits that I discovered in myself are old habits that I need to watch every day if I'm going to make my life more of what I want it to be and my relationships more of what they might be.

• The first one is *worry.* I am a skilled worrier because I have practiced it most of my life. By worrying about tomorrow, I can destroy all the pleasure and enjoyment of even the grandest today. I tend to worry about whether a flat tire might throw our picnic off. I worry that someone I care about might get sick and die. Little things or big things, it doesn't matter, I'm good at worrying about all of them.

Worrying is a technique I've used over many years to implement an attitude that says: *no matter how hard you work or how well you do, the payoff is always going to be unfair and unjust.* Worry is my way of saying "amen" or "so be it" to that bottom-line view of reality. So every day I have to check myself on this score. How did I do today with my old companion? Did I slip into worry three times, but catch myself twice? Good! It was a good day. The point is that if you watch the inches, you never have to watch the miles. What are the inches that *you* need to watch?

• *Projection* is another character defect that I have to watch. I tend to think, "Things would really be good *if* this would happen or *when* so and so happens." Always "if" and "when." Of course, the fact is that I have everything I need for peace of mind *right now* (we all do) and if I can't find it now, I'm not likely to ever find it. That doesn't mean that people who have terrible things going on aren't going to be tempted to project somewhat. But it does mean that if we have sufficient depth of program, of spirituality, life never has to be totally chaotic, miserable, or out of control. It's not a matter of "if" or "when"—it's a matter of "now" or "never." I have to watch the inches on this one.

• I also have to monitor *workaholism.* It's not so much that I work too many hours, but rather that I have learned to get most of my feelings of self-worth by getting results on my projects. Success in my work really pumps me up. For most of my life, *results* have counted for more than anything else. Workaholics are people who need to have their *work* decide whether or not they're going to be happy. So I have to watch that. Do you?

_____'s Program Planner

Habits			
_____	DAILY READING OR INPUT	What	When
_____	SPONSOR/MENTOR	Who	When
_____	GROUP	Where	When
_____	EVALUATION	How	When
_____	PRAYER/MEDITATION	How	When
	HEALTH CARE Recreation Exercise Diet	What	When
	CELEBRATION	What	When

• The last trait I keep track of every day is *my difficulty accepting good things from others.* I don't have a hard time doing good things for others or being readily available when they need me. But I do have a hard time accepting what others give me. And, of course, that is another way of saying that *I don't want to receive* —I want to be in control.

Givers crave control. The people I am giving to obviously need (or at least I think they need) what I have to give. Being a receiver makes me uncomfortable because it means that *I* need something. For a lot of reasons, I have difficulty accepting that I *need* other people and their gifts. And so, for me, the difficulty in giving up control is just another reason why I can't enjoy and make the most of what today offers. If I don't watch it, that becomes a self-fulfilling prophecy.

Your two or three or four habit patterns may be entirely different. If you sincerely want a program that can change things, start thinking about your habits. What is it you need to change? Be as specific and honest as you can—the stakes are high.

Look at the chart on the facing page. This is your Program Planner. Write down on the left-hand side of the chart itself (or copy the chart on a separate sheet of paper) the patterns or habits that you need to deal with. As you write them down, be aware of how much those tyrant habits have cost you. Now look at the rest of the chart and the seven behaviors represented there.

A program is a series of small behaviors that, if practiced consistently, practically, and with focus, will create new alternatives and options for you.

1. Daily Reading or Input

The first behavior listed is daily reading or daily input —any book, tape, record, etc., that gives us new information, new ways to think, a new perspective. Because it's daily, it's disciplined—we see to it every day. Next to daily reading, notice that it says "What" and "When." Fill in what you are using for daily input and when you do it. The point is that if you don't know what you're going to use or when you're going to have time to do it, the chances are good that you *won't* do it.

Why is daily input so important? Because we are talking about changing habits, and the *way we think* is an important element in the structure of our habits. Daily input feeds our minds new ways to think. So what book will you read or tape will you listen to? You may change it from day to day, but you have to know what it is.

Remember that an effective program has to be focused. Look again at the patterns or habits listed on the far left side of your Planner. What kind of input will be most critical to changing those habits? For many people, upbeat, positive input is essential. Many of us need to convince ourselves that we *deserve* the good stuff, and then have it affirmed again and again. Or perhaps we need to learn to set goals. Maybe for most of our lives we've concentrated on survival, not goal-setting. For us, then, one of the many books on setting personal goals, thinking positively, or being your own best friend would be just the ticket for daily input.

As you do your daily reading, focus the input on the patterns or habits that cause you trouble, no matter how unreal or uncomfortable it may feel to be thinking those new thoughts. Concrete and practical— write it down and *do it.*

2. Sponsor or Mentor

Sponsor or mentor is listed next. Across from that it says "Who" and "When." Many people have never truly confided in anyone. But each of us needs someone special, who is chosen very carefully, who we trust, who has no need to elevate us or put us down, and who is farther along the road we're trying to travel. Such people have something to give us and we need to meet and talk with them regularly. *Who* is your mentor?

What do you talk to your sponsor about? What's on the left-hand side of your paper? That's your focus. For almost two years, I met weekly with two sponsors or mentors. They were very different from one another, but each had skills that I was trying to develop. I wanted to find out how they thought. I wanted to know what kind of circuitry was running around in their brains— because obviously their thinking was different than mine, and the results they were getting were much different than mine. I'm not saying that my life was so totally chaotic that there was nothing good about it. Not at all. But parts of my life were causing me too much pain, and I needed to be with people who were walking the path that I wanted to travel. Concrete and practical: who is your mentor or sponsor? If you don't have one now, you'd do yourself a favor to find one. Remember that if you're not willing to do something different, there will be no change. So find that person and write down his or her name.

When are you going to meet? Once a week is certainly not too often if you have someone you think you can really learn from. You may have to ask two or three people before you find someone who is willing to make the commitment, because it really is a commitment. It is a great responsibility to pledge your time, concern, and honesty as a dialogue partner or sponsor over a long period of time. But it is incredibly important to find such people and to share with them regularly—telling them how things are going for you and getting their feedback on how they handled situations similar to those you're facing. The help and love and trust that will develop in that process is worth a thousand times the discomfort it may cause you to initiate such a relationship.

3. Group

The third behavior is group. Do you have a concrete and practical answer to the question, "Where is your group, and when does it meet?" Group is essential. As much as I love and value and trust my mentors and sponsors, they can only give me what they have. Group, however, is a collective experience, drawing on the strength and hope of perhaps twenty or more people. When we meet in group—if the members are really on a journey and not just there to defend where they are and give other people answers—we are part of a totally different experience. We get different wisdom and different input. There is magic in the kind of sharing that can go on in a good group. *Where* does your group meet and *how often* do you go?

4. Evaluation

Evaluation is next. *How* do you do it and *when* do you do it? Members of Twelve Step programs know this kind of evaluation as Tenth Step work—watching the inches on a daily basis so you won't have to deal with the miles. There are many ways to evaluate, but the way that works for me is this: I have written my four negative habit patterns (I call them my demons) on a postcard, which I've taped on the nightstand beside my bed. Every night before I go to sleep I look at that card and say, "OK, how did you do with worry today?" If I had five attacks of worry and dealt with it well only three times, I need to know that. If worry ruined a considerable portion of my day, I need to watch that tomorrow, because if I don't, I'll start to lose more than I'll win. If I don't watch it on a daily basis, it won't take long before I'm right back where I started. How do you do *your* evaluation?

The point, you see, is not to say, "How did I do in general?" but to say, "How did I do with that, that, and that?"—the target habit patterns. Focus your evaluation on those behaviors that have held you down and tripped you up. Look at them right there on the left-hand side of the chart. That's where change is going to take place.

Suppose you listed *insecurity* as one of your habits. Maybe anytime someone looks at you the wrong way or says something different, you get insecure, you get afraid. When you get afraid, you get angry, and when you get angry, you get depressed. If the junkie stays in the driver's seat, that's what chronic insecurity does to people. But if your daily evaluation tells you that four times today you were overwhelmed with the feeling of not being good enough, what can you do with that? How do you deal with it?

Maybe you decide that the time to deal with these old flare-ups is when you do your reading. Or maybe you repeat some slogans to yourself when you're having an attack. Or say a prayer or call your sponsor. Maybe you decide to get with your group more often so you'll have the power to continue on your new path. Evaluation is critical to progress in any realm of your life. If you don't evaluate, you never know for sure how you're doing or where you're going.

5. Prayer and Meditation

Next on the Program Planner is prayer and meditation. Now I'm not talking about religion here. What I'm saying is that, in my opinion, the power of our old, self-defeating ways is so strong that we just can't make it without help. If change is going to happen, we need to tap a source of power that is greater than ourselves. Have you ever tried to use willpower alone to change those things you wrote down? It doesn't work, does it?

Knowing that is part of the conversion experience: *I have done everything I can and it doesn't work.* Obviously, we need more power from somewhere.

One man I know says this phenomenon is like having a jack in your car. Why do you need it? Get a flat tire and you'll find out. The car is too heavy for you to lift, and you simply can't go forward if you have a flat tire! While this hardly says everything there is to say about the higher power, it may be useful for you to think of it as a jack. The higher power can get your car up so you can deal with the flat tire, the habit pattern you're trying to change. So *how* do you get the help of your higher power and *when* do you do it?

There are many, many beautiful books on prayer and meditation. They may not fit you, and I'm not saying that they should, but I am saying that *some form* of regular prayer and meditation is just plain necessary. You can't lift the car otherwise. It's just too heavy. And those flat tires that are your old habits are not going to let you go on. If you don't take care of them, you're *stopped.* So get it in your mind that in some way, your own way, contact has to be established. People with active religious lives may very well incorporate this program practice into a larger, religious framework.

6. Health Care

The sixth behavior on the chart has to do with taking care of yourself physically. Health care has three aspects: exercise, diet, and recreation. So how, when, and where do you take care of your body? Concrete and practical. No matter who you are and how old you are, you are rooted in your body. You *are* your body. If your body is flabby and not in tone, if you are undernourished (which is not to say underfed), you will have a much more difficult time affecting real change. You can't get away from your body.

Let's consider recreation. What do you do for fun? *When* do you have time off for enjoyment? Perhaps you're one of those people who says, "I don't need that kind of stuff," or, "That's for kids," or, "I don't have enough time to do that because I'm always doing things for other people." If you are, maybe you ought to write that attitude down on the left-hand side of your chart. If you don't take any time off, it's no wonder you are always angry and hurt and feeling used. "What do *you* do for recreation?"

It is not healthy to deny yourself time off. But many people don't even know what they might enjoy doing. I'm saying that it's part of your program to find out. What things might be enjoyable to you? Pursuing a hobby? Walking around the lake? Concrete and practical— *what* do you do for fun and *when* do you do it?

Some kind of exercise is crucial. Most of us wouldn't let our houses fall into outrageous disrepair, but we live in our bodies much longer than we live in any house—in a real sense, there is no "home" more personal or worthy of attention than your own body. If we let our bodies become "fixer-uppers," where will we move on *to*? As Tevye said in *Fiddler on the Roof*, "A bird can marry a fish but where will they live?"

I'm not telling you how much or what kind of exercise to get. I'm only making the point that people feel better, think more clearly, and have less stress when they exercise regularly and appropriately.

You and I are more than our minds and emotions and spirits. Each of us is incorporated in a physical being. By learning to think of ourselves as whole persons and by seeing that our problems affect that "whole," we'll see the need for comprehensive solutions. Dealing with our problems holistically means taking good care of our bodies, and that includes exercise.

A healthy diet has more to do with emotional control than with weight control. What we put in our bodies affects our emotions and our nerves. It has often been said, however, that while we are the best-fed country in the world, we're far from the healthiest. We get hooked on caffeine, nicotine, and refined carbohydrates. We ingest pollutants simply by breathing the air and drinking the water. We take too many prescription and over-the-counter drugs. Our bodies need good nutrition to deal with this onslaught.

How about *you*? Are you overfed and undernourished? It's possible, and changing that condition can make a real difference. Remember, if nothing changes, nothing changes. Lots of books and other kinds of information on eating nutritionally are available. Give this matter, along with recreation and exercise, some thought. Concrete and practical—*what* do you do and *when* do you do it?

7. Celebration

The last behavior, which is very important for some people and less so for others, is celebration. This is a crucial daily practice for people who tend to be very hard on themselves. Impatient people, workaholics, and martyrs really *need* to learn to celebrate. We need to practice looking at the successes we have had rather than bewailing and moaning the distance we have yet to go. There is no end to the journey of human growth, and that fact is surely cause for celebration. The potential of human beings to be healthy and whole and happy is almost limitless.

Concrete and practical—if you are the kind of person who really needs to celebrate, pat your own back, give yourself a break—*what* do you do and *when* do you do it? Make sure your celebration doesn't always revolve around food, especially junk food. And it shouldn't always require spending money, either. It may be simply taking time off to read something you've been wanting to read or to listen to a record. You must make time —time is your *gift* to yourself.

Some people, however, were born to celebrate. They are good at it. For them, the seventh behavior might involve doing something for someone else every day. Think about that. You may find that a year has gone by without your ever, consciously, having done something for someone else. Know yourself! What is on the left-hand side of your chart?

If you have filled out your chart, you now have a program tailor-made for yourself. You may choose some of the suggested behaviors and reject others. It's your program. It's your life. Now at least you know what to do. This is the schedule and these are the small, "doable" things that will *change your life* if you make them practical, concrete, focused, and consistent. There is no way that change will *not* happen if you focus your program on the patterns or habits that cause you the most trouble.

As much as anyone in this world, *you* deserve to change. You deserve to be happy. Everyone does. You know what you will gain if you do effect the change and you know what you will lose if you don't. And you know how to do it. The building blocks are yours. You are the architect and the mason. If you want to travel the road of Stage II Recovery and build yourself a castle— create it. Then move in and enjoy it.

Recap

1. The third step of change is action—or working a program of change.
2. An effective program is concrete, practical, focused, and consistent.

3. A good program involves a small series of behaviors that, if done consistently, create new life options.

4. Some of the small behaviors that constitute a program may include daily reading or input, a sponsor or mentor, group, evaluation, prayer or meditation, health care, and celebration.

A blessed thing it is for any man or woman
to have a friend,
one human soul whom we can trust utterly,
who knows the best and worst of us,
and who loves us in spite of our faults.
                                        —Anonymous

Of all sad words of tongue or pen
the saddest are these, "It might have been."
                            —John Greenleaf Whittier

No one has love. Love exists between two poles creating at both
ends.
                                        —Martin Buber

6

RELATIONSHIPS

In focusing on relationships, we come full circle in our consideration of Stage II Recovery. Whether they're with a spouse, friends, children, co-workers, group members, or our higher power, our relationships are the mirrors that reflect our truest selves. Nothing is more central to Stage II Recovery than increasing our ability to function in loving, rewarding relationships.

So what kinds of connections are we making now and how can we make them better? And how does this focus on relationships fit in with the personal change I'm trying to effect by working my program?

The self-defeating learned behaviors we've been talking about are part of *who we are* as friend, parent, significant other, group member, and child of God. We can bring no other self to these roles. Remember that we have been training all our lives to be who we are. So in a sense we have been working a program all along, although it's probably not a conscious one. Now that we are creating new visions and new pathways, we will need to practice the same kind of repetitious program to develop the new skills.

How badly do you need new relationship skills? Let's take a look.

Up Close and Personal

Considering the habits you identified earlier, think about their effect on your ability to function in relationships.

1. HABIT TO BE CHANGED:_____

Perhaps you wrote something like this: *I tend to think I am always right, and that I know what is best. If people would do what I know they should, everything would be fine.*

Caretakers often have such thoughts. Can this kind of thinking cause problems in relationships?

Remember that who you are in a relationship *with* says as much about you as it does about them. It follows, then, that Caretakers will only be in relationships with people who allow them to act out their patterns. In general, while there are a wide variety of Caretakers, most will take control and responsibility in a relationship because they need the ultimate say-so.

Caretakers often find themselves playing a kind of game called "Genius-to-Idiot." That is, they feel comfortable communicating *from* a genius position to an idiot position. If I am the genius because I always need

to be right, then you must be the idiot. When I communicate in this fashion, I am saying, "We'll only talk about
this for as long as it takes me to convince you that I am
right. I'm not really listening to you. I'm just waiting
for you to stop talking so I can affirm what I know to be
the truth."

Has anyone ever played the "Genius-to-Idiot" game
with you? If so, take some time and jot down your reactions to the experience. How do you handle it when a
genius communicates to you that way? Here are some of
the ways that people have played the idiot role. See if
any of them sound familiar:

- "I get mad, but then I just shut up. She always thinks
  she won, but I always get even."
- "If he wants to correct me—I make sure he has plenty
  of complaints to work with."
- "I might not know as much as she thinks *she* does, but I
  never give her an inch. I fight her every step of the
  way."
- "Even if he is right, I don't admit it. I just say, 'Why
  ask me? You think you know everything. Just do
  whatever you want.' "

The anatomy of a failed relationship often reveals
games built upon games, self-defeating learned behaviors playing against self-defeating learned behaviors.
The process becomes a spiraling descent into distrust.

We can't control another person's willingness to work
a program and stop behaving in distrustful, disrespect-
ful ways towards others. We can only control ourselves.
If Caretakers are not willing to take a good look at
themselves and effect some change, there simply won't
be any change. Because they don't see it, Caretakers
may be amazed when the same patterns develop again
and again in their lives. Wherever they go, they will
find themselves acting out the same dynamics. And
they may well be mystified until the day they die.

2. HABIT TO BE CHANGED:_____

Did you put down something like this? *I have a terrible time standing up for myself. I often say yes when I want to say no. If only people would stop asking so much of me.*

People-Pleasers habitually think this way. Can this pattern cause trouble in relationships? Let us count the ways!

People-Pleasers often find themselves in games like "You Decide." People-Pleasers, of course, hate to make decisions. If they do, they might make a mistake, and when you make mistakes, someone gets mad at you--at least in the People-Pleaser's world. And if people get mad at you, so the Guardian says, they will go away and you'll be left all alone, which is what you deserve because you aren't worth much anyway.

Habits create needs. Therefore, People-Pleasers nearly always find themselves in relationships with abusers of one kind or another, people who like the idea of having someone around to put down. The game begins when the partner tries to put the burden of decision on the People-Pleaser. After all, if it is the wrong decision, the partner certainly doesn't want to take the blame.

"Should we go to the show?" "I don't care, you decide." "Should we buy a new house?" "I don't know. You decide." "Should we paint the kitchen?" "Who knows! You decide." "Should we fix the hole in the floor so we stop falling through?" "There you go again. How do I know? If you want it fixed, you decide. You do it."

It doesn't take a mastermind to figure out that if the decision is "wrong" or if the abuser just wants something to holler about, the People-Pleaser is going to get it in the neck. No matter what he or she does, it is wrong. No matter how obvious it is that the task needs doing, if the People-Pleaser does it, he or she will be punished for it. In this situation, both people lose.

Primary, Stage I Recovery may well get us out of a bad place, but it doesn't get us to a good one. A clean People-Pleaser is still a People-Pleaser. Stage I Recovery deals with the immediate problem at hand, but only Stage II Recovery gets at the underlying patterns and habits that caused us trouble in the first place. If nothing changes, nothing changes. And if nothing changes, the same results will pop up through our whole life.

Has anyone ever played the "You-Decide" game on you? If so, how did you respond? Here are some classic reactions:

• "I got to where I wouldn't do anything. Everything seemed easier that way. If there was a hole in the floor —well, fall through. I'm not going to do anything about it."

• "I get terribly mad and throw things, but then I feel even crazier than I did before I threw them."

• "I can't outtalk him so I make cynical remarks about anything he cares about. Which isn't much."

• "I don't say anything."

There is no guarantee that if one person changes by working a program the other will change, too. No one can change for another person. But if People-Pleasers are ever going to share in increasingly rewarding relationships, they must work their program and stop acting out that pattern.

3. HABIT TO BE CHANGED:_____

Maybe you put down something like this: *I tend to be preoccupied with work. I am always busy, so busy that people get in the way of my progress. Sometimes I figure out ways of not going home so I can get more done at work.*

Workaholics often think like this. How does this pattern get in the way of successful relationships?

Workaholics may communicate to their loved ones that they count, but just not as much as the "real stuff."

Partners of Workaholics always live in a state of rejection. They feel second best. Cheated. Or, as one woman told me, "I don't even make the top ten."

Workaholics often get caught up in a game called "Wait Till I'm Done."

- "Can we take a walk now?"
  "Wait till I'm done with this report."
- "Can we talk about Billy's grades now?"
  "Wait till I'm finished painting this bookcase."
- "When are we going to take our vacation?"
  "Wait till I finish the next project."

I have worked with many Workaholics over the years. Some were in a Twelve Step Program and some were not. But nothing got better for any of them until they started seriously looking at their patterns, Guardians and all, and began working a program.

Marriage after marriage, or fight after fight in the same marriage, the same patterns bubbled to the top and periodically blew the lid off the relationship. Until these people moved into Stage II, they could never understand why the other person was so "unreasonable." One man even asked me, "Why can't she just wait her turn?"

How have you responded when someone played the "Wait-Till-I'm-Done" game? Again, some common reactions:

- "I stopped asking him to participate and just did my own thing."
- "I got to hate his friends. I put them down every chance I got."
- "I got terribly jealous of her work. I hate everything I get jealous of. So I got to hate her work and never gave her any support or affirmation about what she was doing."

Down, down the relationships go till there is nothing left to build on. Each side fortifies itself behind a wall of righteousness and so it stays.

Workaholics will never find peace or growth in their lives until they are willing to take a hard look at themselves and the self-defeating habits that destroy their healthy relationships.

4. HABIT TO BE CHANGED:_____

Suppose you wrote down something like this: *I never have fun. Nothing ever seems to work out right for me. I do without for so many people, but no one ever seems willing to give to me in return.*

Martyrs think a lot like this. How do Martyrs self-destruct in relationships?

Again, since habits create needs, Martyrs seldom find themselves in situations that *could* work out. Or, if the possibility is there, they soon find a way to make sure it gets squashed.

Martyrs often participate in a game called "Let's Awfulize." "Awfulizing" is a technique that makes any irregularity in life a disaster. Things we need aren't just expensive, they "will put us in the poor house." The parking lot isn't full, it "is so crowded, we'll have to walk five miles." A place isn't far, it's "at the end of the world." The road between here and there isn't bumpy, it's "so bad we'll probably break an axle and not get there at all."

A skillful but recovering Martyr once told me that as a child, when her family was driving somewhere, if one of the kids asked, "How long till we get there?" the standard answer was, "Who knows *if* we'll get there?"

Awfulizers not only maximize anything bad that might happen, but minimize everything good. For them, the best that anything can be is "nice." Have you ever tried to have fun with an Awfulizer? Have you ever tried to relax or celebrate or play with a Martyr? Depending on the depth of the habit, it can't be done at all or, at best, only to a very limited degree.

I have frequently heard people talk about how happy their lives could have been if only the Martyr would have let it be so. How short life is, they say, and how sad it is to waste so much precious time contemplating disaster.

Here are some typical responses people make to the Awfulizer:

- "I cry a lot."
- "I just get mad and demand that he stop saying such stupid stuff."
- "I go out alone and do all the fun things I can. For some reason, she just can't share in it. It makes me feel bad, but what else can I do?"

Wherever Martyrs go, they find ample reason to awfulize and feel disappointed in what they find. But it isn't "out there" that has to change. The only way a real, inner change happens is by working your own, concrete, practical, focused, consistent program.

5. HABIT TO BE CHANGED:_____

Suppose you wrote something like this: *Mistakes drive me crazy. I hate anything disorderly or out of place. I have a need to demand perfection from myself and everyone around me.*

Perfectionists habitually think along these lines. Since Perfectionists demand perfection and since nothing can ever be perfect, especially relationships, these people can obviously never be happy. And neither can those who find themselves in relationships with Perfectionists.

Perfectionists like to play a game called "It Could Have Been a Little Better." This message is not always delivered in words—it's an attitude that pervades everything the Perfectionist sees and touches. No achievement is ever quite impressive enough. Good grades are never really *that* good, and if they are, it's because the competition was poor. A competent performance always lacks brilliance, a tasty meal lacks the gourmet touch, and the prettiest day always has a little too much wind. Nothing and no one is ever quite good enough. What is wrong is the first thing noted in everyone and everything.

Perfectionists are terribly hard to live with, and self-esteem takes a terrible beating at their hands. Because they can't accept the flaws themselves, everything is seen as flawed and, therefore, unacceptable. No praise is ever pure, no compliment is ever given without reservation. And as with all these habits, we aren't talking about bad people who are intentionally being nasty. This is truly the way Perfectionists see reality. It is the way they see themselves. To them, "it could have been a little better" makes all the sense in the world. It isn't a game, it's reality. Until they, we, all of us, "hit the wall" hard enough to alter our perceptions, we have no choice but to act out the reality we see.

If you have ever been in a relationship with a Perfectionist, how have you tended to respond? Here are some examples I've come across:

• "I quit trying to do anything 'right,' since that's obviously impossible in his eyes."

• "She thinks she's so good. I just got to where all I do is point out *her* faults when she tells me I haven't done something well enough."

• "I've become afraid to try anything because I hate to hear how incapable I am. So I do nothing, and I don't feel good about it."

The patterns go round and round until there is a conversion experience and a corresponding program is put into effect. All of us think that we are totally in touch with reality and that our behavior is perfectly appropriate. And so we are—in touch with *our* reality. Obeying *our* Guardian. In Stage II Recovery, we deal with those habits that live on long after our primary addiction has been broken.

6. HABIT TO BE CHANGED:_____

Suppose you wrote something like this: *Commitments scare me to death, so I never really take a stand. I have a lot of trouble knowing how I feel, let alone telling anybody else about it.*

Tap Dancers think like this and act like this. Of all people, Tap Dancers are perhaps the most difficult to be in relationships with because you never know if they're going to be there for you or not. At one moment they seem to want something firm in a relationship. But when you follow up on that assumption, you find it isn't what they meant at all. They aren't "there" anymore. They're somewhere else.

Tap Dancers may make love to you, take you on trips, and give you expensive gifts, all of which seem to say, "This is solid. This is where I want to be." But they seem totally mystified or even angry when you suggest that you need some exclusivity or a deeper commitment from them.

A favorite game of Tap Dancers is "Don't Fence Me In." It is sometimes said that they live in round houses so they can never be cornered. Because they have such a need for love and intimacy, as we all do, they always seem to be in relationships—many of them, and at the same time. In each relationship, they are willing to appear committed, to act committed, and to sound committed. As soon as they sense that the corral door may be shutting, they bolt for freedom. Don't fence me in.

Are they bad people? Do Tap Dancers get a kick out of breaking someone's heart? Not at all. They are merely acting out reality as they see it. They are steering clear of a confrontation with their Guardian, as we all do until there is a compelling enough reason to go to war.

If you have ever danced with a Tap Dancer, you have probably played "don't fence me in." How have you responded?

- "I thought he always backed off because there was something wrong with me. So I tried harder to show him that I loved him."
- "I cried. Then got mad. Then got hurt. Then cried again."
- "I got to where I never trusted a thing she said."
- "I got fed up and demanded a commitment. If he won't give it, I'll tell him to 'take a hike.' "

After we trot out all the principles and guidelines and examples, the secret of effective, loving relationships is probably revealed as clearly in the following little story as it is anywhere. This is a story of heaven and hell.

A crowd of very hungry people was called in to the banquet room. They were delighted to see a long table piled high with wonderful food in the center of the room. As the people approached the table, each one was presented with a spoon with an extremely long handle. The handle was so long, in fact, that it was impossible to get the spoon into your mouth.

Since everybody had been called to the same banquet, the difference between heaven and hell was neither the spoon, nor the food, nor the hunger. The difference was that the people in hell ended up starving because the long spoon handles wouldn't let them feed themselves, while the people in heaven simply fed each other.

The risk, of course, is that we may feed someone who is not trustworthy and will not feed us in return. If that happens, we lose, and ultimately they do, too. *Both of us are denied heaven by our own hand.* But if we *do* feed each other, neither of us need ever be hungry again.

Recap

1. Nothing is more central to Stage II Recovery than increasing our ability to function in loving, rewarding relationships.

2. The first step in building new relationships is to be willing to take a look at me, not you.

3. Taking a look at me means identifying and dealing with the self-defeating learned behaviors that prohibit me from having more honest relationships.

Nothing happens unless first a dream.
　　　　　—Carl Sandburg

It ain't over 'til it's over.
　　　　　—Yogi Berra

Some people feel the rain, others just get wet.
　　　　　—Roger Miller

7

SUCCESS

Since this book began with a flight of the mind to all the different kinds of Twelve Step meetings going on around the world, it seems fitting to conclude with a similar visit to some of the hundreds of thousands of lives that have been lit with the glow of Stage II Recovery.

Do you remember the story I told about the young couple and their baby? They approached me after church, you may recall, amid all the hustle and bustle of the crowd. With shining eyes, these two proud parents, who are both paying the price of Stage II Recovery and enjoying its unique rewards, held out their child and said, "The cycle stops here." I knew that they had thought this moment out thoroughly, and I was deeply touched.

Both people knew all too well the demons of fear and insecurity that haunt the world of nonrecovery. They had spent some hard time dealing with doubt and frustration as they started their climb up into the light. They had been there and they knew. They knew all about the fierce, silent battles that need to be waged in the "walled-up fortress of the heart" if true freedom is ever to be gained. Once fought, those battles leave their scars upon the face and eyes, so that a fellow pilgrim, passing by, recognizes and knows, without words, that you know.

Ruth and Paul know those struggles, and they know the birthplace of those struggles as well—their self-defeating learned behaviors. Dents. Dents lived with, learned, and practiced. Dents no doubt created without malice, but dents all the same. Dents in need of repair.

Neither of these young parents presumes perfection. Both know that dents are a part of life—a necessary part. They have too much wisdom to assume that they will do a perfect job of parenting. In saying, "The cycle stops here," they were saying, "What we know, we can teach. Who we are, we can model. As far as we are able, and now we are much more able, we will spare this child the worst of the dents. As he goes through life, this child may walk taller and straighter because of what we are now able to offer. He may have the marvelous advantage of looking into a mirror and liking what he sees. He may make a friend of silence for he will not be afraid to hear his own song."

In that moment, for it was just a moment, there was a fluttering of angel wings. For when all is said and done, where the analysis is completed and the teaching is organized, what it is all about is the preciousness of life. All we are talking about in Stage II Recovery is learning to walk straighter and taller. Ultimately, Stage II Recovery is about the ability to hear the flutter of angel's wings.

All around us, there are countless quiet moments of spiritual growth unfolding. Here are some examples of the beauty of Stage II Recovery that have been shared with me. Can you hear the flutter?

*

"I had to admit that the relationship I was in was bad for me. By working my program, I hope to meet someone who is capable of being trustworthy."

*

"Anybody can make a mistake, but no one has to make the same mistake over and over and over, the way I have. I need to keep on myself every day to make a difference. It's hard, but I believe in my own future."

*

"A lot of times I'm not comfortable, but by thinking positively and going ahead, I'm achieving what I want for myself."

*

"I am a Caretaker and my husband is a Workaholic/Perfectionist. We have learned to be patient with ourselves and with each other as we try to change. We have grown."

*

"My search for a signficant other is more self- assured, and my time with myself has become more serene. For the first time, I feel adequate."

*

"Only last week I realized that I'm *worth* changing. That was a big step for me. It really opened my eyes."

*

"I'm more able to give my husband and children more of the good that is inside me. There's a lot more to do, but at least we've broken ground."

*

'I've become more serious about taking care of myself first and not taking responsibility for how others react. I am now aware of where I am stuck."

*

"I realize now that I'm a grown adult and no longer have to be the child I was. I'm a good person."

*

"I'm laughing more now and being a different kind of person with my kids."

*

"I'm more sensitive to other people. I feel their happiness and sadness. Before, I never let myself."

*

"In the past I did some crazy things just for attention. Now I know I was just looking for love. I'm learning not to be so defensive so people can get close to me."

*

"I'm happy to find out that there are others who feel as I do. I'm amazed that there seems to be a way out."

*

"I wrote an assets list and debits list about myself. It made me feel good that the assets outweighed the debits."

*

"I'm not as scared of life. I feel OK now about being without a girlfriend. My Doom Syndrome seems to be going away."

*

"I've been acting as if I didn't have a choice. Now I'm taking charge of my destiny and becoming willing to look at some things I can do."

*

"I realize that I've bought some stuff from my parents that I don't want. I've always refused to see it, but now I think I can make some of my own decisions."

*

"It's only now, almost six years to the day that I took my last drink, that my need for more intimacy in relationships sort of hit me in the face. I'm trying to learn to trust."

*

"I've applied, 'If nothing changes, nothing changes,' to almost every area of my life—work, kids, and my house. It helps keep me honest."

*

"I'm working on living in the present. When my family comes home, I stop what I'm doing for a minute to be open to them."

*

"I'm starting to challenge some things that other people tell me. I'm starting to say, 'I feel _____,' and sometimes even to say, 'I don't have the answer.' "

*

"I've learned that I'm a worthwhile person—even if I don't have the attributes that I envy in someone else."

*

"I'm in touch with some feelings that haven't surfaced for a long time. I feel OK about it."

*

"When my kids don't want me to go out to my meetings, I tell them I'm going because I love them. I know that I deserve some help and that I don't have to feel guilty."

*

"I've decided to enjoy my life rather than waste it. I've bought myself some new clothes and I'm going to take a trip with my sister. I can't believe it's me doing this."

*

"I'm learning to say no and to stand up for myself even though I may get the cold shoulder for awhile. I'm not letting my alcoholic father lay guilt trips on me anymore."

*

"I ended a bad relationship a few months ago and I'm still struggling to let go emotionally. But everyday I'm learning, and I've already gone much farther than I ever thought I could."

*

"I have shared what I've learned with my boss and have given him notice that I want and deserve respect. I won't be talked down to any longer."

*

"I grew up with the idea that nothing was good except work, work, work. So I worked. Now I'm taking time for relaxing."

*

"I thought a lot of things about myself could never be fixed. Now I'm really trying to fix them. It's exciting."

*

"Sometimes I have days that are really good and happy. Now I'm not willing to put up with the kind of days that drag me down."

*

"My wife and I are coming together in a 'real' relationship for the first time in seventeen years."

*

"Six months ago I had a breakdown and was hospitalized. I don't ever want to feel that way again, so I'm working hard. I have come a long way and I'm proud of it."

*

"I don't know all the answers but I feel good about the direction I'm taking. Blaming or taking the blame has become unimportant."

*

"I was afraid to share my weakness with my wife. If anything, this process has made us grow closer. The risk was worth taking."

*

"Basically, I seem to get out of my slumps quicker and get back into a positive frame of mind."

*

"I can now act without despair. I feel like I've joined the ranks of the living."

*

"I'm not as selfish as I used to be. I care more. As a supervisor at work, I've been able to help people."

*

"I know I'm getting better when I can cry if I feel sad, when I can laugh at myself, and when I can listen to my family."

*

"I used to accept responsibility for my family's happiness or sadness but it was very hard to be 'perfect' for someone else all the time. I'm much happier now that I don't have to do that anymore."

*

"By talking to other people and writing things down I feel like I have an outlet for my emotions that have only been in my head. I feel happier and less confused."

*

"I'm starting to listen to myself instead of trying to guess what other people think I should do. I've made some decisions."

*

"I still feel rage when I think of certain events of the past that I handled so poorly. But I'm learning to stop those tapes by understanding how I got there and how I can get away."

*

"I've learned that I don't have to play the role of the victim and that I can take initiative and change my life."

*

"The love and closeness I feel, when I'm able to let my walls down and not play my games, is great. I want more, so I'm continuing to work my program."

*

"Even though it's not easy, I feel new inner strength as I take control of my life. I've made some drastic changes and it's a wonder that I'm not an emotional wreck, but I'm not."

*

"It may be a rocky road for a long time, but I'm moving in a more productive, self-respecting direction from now on."

*

"I discovered why I've related to people the way I have, and that I am the one who caused my relationships to be shallow. I've taken definite steps to change that situation."

*

"I'm beginning to learn to experience love and attention from my partner as a gift to me. This helps me to know giving as a pleasure without anticipation and anxiety."

*

"When old family arguments start, I can stop myself and say, 'Not again! We don't have to do this anymore!' It is difficult not to give in to the old thoughts, the old programming, but it can be done!"

*

"I'm better equipped now to know myself in the context of 'now' rather than in the context of those who have influenced me in the past."

*

"It's helped me a lot to find out what kind of person I am. I've usually felt helpless and undeserving, but now I feel ready to be happy. I'm allowing myself to have close friends. It's beautiful to be loved!"

*

"There's a closeness in my relationship that wasn't there before. Communication is better, and I'm still looking for improvement."

*

"I'm more aware of how I respond to people. I'm also trying to be more in touch with myself and what is important to me."

*

"I started college! I didn't think I could do that because fear of my failure. I have better self-esteem now."

*

"I've been told before that a lot of people share my experience of growing up in a 'not-so-perfect' family. I believed it, but it's a whole other thing to actually experience it. I know I'm not alone."

*

"I can talk better with my family, and I'm noticing things that I do and say that must be changed. I've told my dad that I'm out to help myself."

*

"I now have hope for a sane relationship. By being honest, I can become whole enough to break some of my crazy patterns."

*

"I tend to be very negative and insecure about myself. By keeping a journal, I've discovered that I have been 'forbidden' to do anything for myself. I'm changing this now."

*

"I don't let other people determine my moods anymore. Best of all, I don't feel guilty about it."

*

"I accept myself as I am—the good and the bad. I am a neat person even though I have rough edges."